KU-021-985

# DISCOVERING
# BIRDS

# DISCOVERING
# BIRDS

## A guide to over 250 British and European species
### Identification · Habitats · Behaviour

# JIM FLEGG

Hamlyn

LONDON · NEW YORK · SYDNEY · TORONTO

# Acknowledgements

## Illustrations
Habitat colour plates by David Thompson and Mick Loats/Linden Artists
Identification illustrations by Ian Willis,
with additional material by Brin Edwards/Format Publishing Services
Line illustrations by David Webb/Linden Artists

## Photographic Acknowledgements

While every effort has been made to obtain permission for the publication of all copyright material it is possible that we may inadvertently have failed to obtain the necessary permission. In all cases we offer our apologies to the copyright owners.

AFA (Geoffrey Kinns); Heather Angel; Aquila Photographics (A. J. Bond, D. Green, H. A. Hems, H. Kinloch, T. Leach, W. S. Paton, E. K. Thompson, M. C. Wilkes); Archivio Fotografico Longo; Ardea Photographics (J. A. Bailey, B. Bevan, J. C. Blewitt, J. B. & S. Bottomley, K. Carlson, W. Curth, M. D. England, C. R. Knights, P. R. Messent, R. Vaughan, J. Wightman); Jen & Des Bartlett; Black Star (Pickford); Frank V. Blackburn; J. B. & S. Bottomley; L. H. Brown; Dr Kevin J. Carlson; Arthur Christiansen; Bruce Coleman Ltd (Frank V. Blackburn, Rodney Dawson, Peter Hinchcliffe, G. Langsbury, J. Markham, D. Middleton, A. Morgan, W. J. C. Murray, S. C. Porter, H. Reinhard, G. Ziesler); D. A. P. Cooke; Stephen Dalton; Adrian Davies; C. de Klemm; A. J. Deane; Ernest Duscher; M. D. England; Jim Flegg; Robert Gillmor; David A. Gowans; Jan Grahn; Dennis Green; D. W. Greenslade; R. H. Hallam; N. W. Harwood; Roy A. Harris & K. R. Duff; Dennis W. Hatton; Brian Hawkes; Urpo Hayrinen; Urdo Hirsch; Ingmar Holmasen; David Hosking; Eric Hosking; Jacana (Brosselin, Herze Chaumeton, J. Dubois, Ducrot, B. Hawkes, C. de Klemm, J. C. Maes, Mallet, Montoya, C. Nardin, Jacques Robert, Varin, Albert Visage); E. A. Janes; Edgar T. Jones; M. Philip Kahl; Frank Lane (Christiansen, Norman Duerden, F. Merlet; G. T. H. Moon, George Quedens, W. Schrempp, R. Thompson, D. Zingel); Gordon Langsbury; John Markham; Derek Middleton; Richard T. Mills; Christopher K. Mylne; National Collection of Nature Photographs, Ottawa (Dr D. F. Parmelee); Natural History Photographic Agency (F. V. Blackburn, A. Butler, D. N. Dalton, S. Dalton, B. Hawkes, E. A. Janes, J. Jeffery, Walter J. C. Murray, P. Scott); Nature Photographers (R. Tidman, Don Smith); Carl E. Ostman (I. Holmasen); Alan Parker; Klaus Paysan; A. N. H. Peach; S. C. Porter; George Quedens; S. Roberts; J. Robinson; Royal Society for the Protection of Birds; Reinhard Siegel; Robert T. Smith; P. O. Swanberg; Jan Van de Kam; Joseph van Wormer; Richard Vaughan; H. J. Verdon; Iikka Virkkunen; J. Wagstaff; John Warham; We Ha Photo, Berne (Max Berger); J. S. Wightman; Wildlife Studies Ltd; Herbert Zettl; Gunther Ziesler
Front jacket: Barn owls (Tyto alba) – Bruce Coleman Ltd/Hans Reinhard
Back jacket: Kittiwakes (Rissa tridactyla), guillemots (Uria aalge) and shags (Phalacrocorax aristotelis) on cliff face – David Hosking.

Published by The Hamlyn Publishing Group Limited
London · New York · Sydney · Toronto
Astronaut House, Feltham, Middlesex, England.

Copyright © The Hamlyn Publishing Group Limited 1984

All rights reserved. No part of this publication may
be reproduced, stored in a retrieval system, or transmitted,
in any form or by any means, electronic, mechanical,
photocopying, recording or otherwise, without the permission
of The Hamlyn Publishing Group Limited.

*Some of the illustrations in this book are reproduced from other books
published by The Hamlyn Publishing Group Limited*

ISBN 0 600 30605 4

Printed in Spain

# Contents

# Introduction

The chief aims of this book are twofold: firstly to allow identification to be made of the majority of the common species of birds to be found in Britain and Europe, and secondly to give the reader an understanding not only of the more interesting aspects of birds' lives, but also to show how they, like all living things, play an integral part in their chosen habitat, and how each is adapted to its way of life.

Birds are to be found almost everywhere, from the most remote mountain top to the heart of the busiest city or the middle of the widest ocean, and this, their sheer abundance, must be a major part of the attraction they hold for man. A wide variety of species are both numerous and colourful, and many are approachable in daylight to such a degree that we are *all* familiar with at least some birds. Man has always been fascinated by birds, and they feature in some of the earliest of Stone Age man's cave paintings. The owls have been revered for their wisdom since ancient Athenian times, and ibises were sacred items in Egyptian burials at the time of the Pharaohs. Even today, a special aura of 'nobility' surrounds birds of prey such as the golden eagle or the peregrine, because of their superb hunting skills and aloof bearing. There is also the aesthetic aspect of birds to consider, for they are widely appreciated not only for their individual beauty, but also for the overall role they play in nature. Rooks flighting to roost against a farmland sunset, for example, or a skein of geese in V-formation against the sky above an estuary, are memorable sights in the countryside. The daily lives and ecology of birds are fascinating, too, and these are far easier to observe than in any other group of animals.

In most people's minds, the word 'bird' is instantly linked with 'flight', for although other animals have achieved the power of flight – insects, bats and some gliding mammals – none can demonstrate the same mastery of the air. Although flight is not unique to birds, the feathers that enable them to fly so expertly certainly are. Feathers also keep birds warm by providing both an underlayer of insulating down and a covering of windproof, streamlined and often also waterproof body feathers. Additionally, feathers may give camouflage or may be used for visual communication in various displays.

## EVOLUTION AND EXPANSION

Birds branched off from their ancestral reptilian stock at approximately the same time as the mammals, over 130 million years ago. Although both birds and mammals have warm blood, unlike their ancestors, it is quite clear from examining a variety of anatomical features that the two groups of animals are quite distinct, and that birds today are more closely related to reptiles than they are to mammals.

The birds' ability to fly enabled them to expand their range and exploit all types of habitats: oceans, forests, mountains and even deserts. This has led to the extraordinary phenomenon known as migration, where seasonally abundant food sources in remote parts of the globe can be swiftly and efficiently exploited, the migrants returning to more stable areas when the climate becomes inhospitable. Thus birds have been seen in practically every area of the globe, virtually from pole to pole, and at heights in excess of that of Mount Everest, over 29,000 ft (8800 m) high. There are, however, limitations: only rarely have birds been found to penetrate more than 30 ft (10 m) into the earth's crust, and each year some part of their lives must be spent in contact with land – for birds cannot build nests at sea – even though some freshwater species build floating nests and only rarely step on to dry land.

The varied lifestyles of birds are reflected in the strikingly different shapes of their feathers.

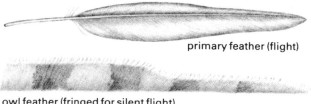

primary feather (flight)

owl feather (fringed for silent flight)

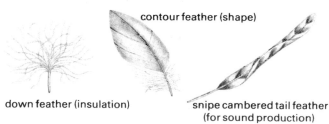

contour feather (shape)

down feather (insulation)

snipe cambered tail feather (for sound production)

## HOW BIRDS ARE CLASSIFIED

If you look at a chaffinch and a goldfinch, it is easy to see they are related. They have very similar body and beak shapes, and behave in a similar way. Nevertheless in the wild they never interbreed. We can recognize them as distinct from each other, and so can they. A number of factors prevent interbreeding, of which one is plumage. A chaffinch recognizes only the plumage colours and patterns of another chaffinch when selecting its mate, and the courtship display reinforces this. A displaying male goldfinch would not attract a female chaffinch. There are ecological barriers, too; goldfinches are birds of heath and scrub, while chaffinches are woodland birds, so the two rarely meet. We therefore have two distinct groups of birds – chaffinches and goldfinches – which do not interbreed, for a variety of reasons, with other groups. Each of these groups is called a species.

If a species occurs over a wide geographical area, then often small local variations in colour, size or song may arise. These subgroups are called subspecies (or sometimes races). Usually the barrier separating them from others of their species is a mountain range, a desert, or a sea. Most birdwatchers would be able to detect differences in song between, for instance, the various subspecies of chaffinches which exist in the Mediterranean area, northern Europe, and the British Isles, and these differences have arisen due to the barriers imposed by the Alps and the English Channel.

The process of evolution has ensured that each species is suited to its particular portion of a habitat. Any variants which occur do not survive long, for they cannot compete successfully for food and nesting sites. If the niche changes, however, then one of these variants might have a better chance of survival. This could mean that, in the course of time, a new species might develop. It is likely that two of the most confusing pairs of species that birdwatchers are likely to encounter, the chiffchaff and willow warbler, and the willow tit and marsh tit, have recently undergone this long-drawn-out evolutionary process.

Bird names can be very confusing, too. For example, the bird known as the robin in the U.S.A. is very different from the familiar robin of Europe. Early American colonists saw a red-breasted thrush, and out of nostalgia for their homeland they called it 'robin'. Such misuse of names causes problems when we watch birds worldwide, and to overcome this each species of bird – and indeed each living creature – has a scientific (Latin) name which is used throughout the world in fieldguides and other books.

Specialist taxonomists and ornithologists throughout the world have worked out the relationships of all the birds, and have grouped them together. Closely related species are placed in the same genus. So the black tern *Chlidonias niger* (*niger* meaning black) joins the white-winged black tern *Chlidonias leucopterus* (*leuco* meaning white, and *pterus* meaning wing) in the genus *Chlidonias*. The first part of the name – in this instance *Chlidonias* – always refers to the genus, and the second part refers to the species. Related genera are grouped in families – so *Chlidonias* (the marsh terns) joins *Sterna* (the sea terns) and *Larus* (the gulls) in the family Laridae, which contains 82 different species. Similarly, the family Laridae is grouped, with other families of seabirds, in the order Charadriiformes. All the various orders of birds make up the class Aves (the birds), and the class Aves is one of several comprising the vertebrate animals, which also includes fishes, reptiles and mammals.

There are several races of the yellow wagtail throughout Europe, each with its distinctive plumage. These are thought to have evolved when populations of birds became isolated from each other by geographical features such as mountain ranges.

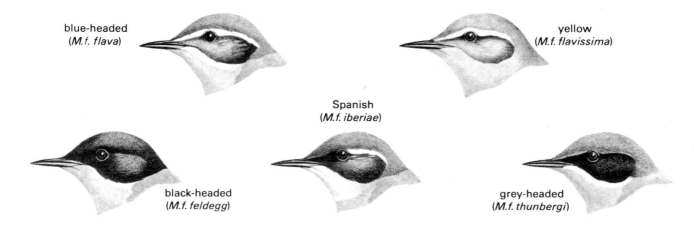

blue-headed
(*M.f. flava*)

yellow
(*M.f. flavissima*)

Spanish
(*M.f. iberiae*)

black-headed
(*M.f. feldegg*)

grey-headed
(*M.f. thunbergi*)

# Bird anatomy

In the 130 million years or so during which birds have existed as a separate class of animals, they have retained their basic structure to a remarkable extent. Compared with most other groups of animals, even the most outwardly different birds resemble each other closely internally. This means that, for instance, similarly derived bones exist in the wings of both hummingbirds and ostriches, and in the feet of hawks and ducks.

During the course of evolution, these limbs have been modified for different purposes. The wing of the hummingbird is perhaps the most efficient organ of flight in the animal kingdom, enabling the bird to perform aerial movements up, down, sideways, forwards and even backwards, and allowing it to remain stationary whilst hovering in front of a nectar-rich flower. The wing of the ostrich, a bird which cannot fly, is used as an organ of balance and display, and as a cooling fan during the hot African day. Throughout the bird families numerous other examples of wing designs can be seen, each suited to the various adopted life-styles: the sickle-shaped wings of the swift, built for speed, are matched by those of the hobby falcon, fast enough on the wing to catch even the swift; the broad wings of the buzzard are built for energy-saving soaring; and the rounded, scoop-shaped wings of the partridge are designed to give instant powerful lift to assist quick escape from a predator.

The feet of birds have also evolved into a variety of shapes for different uses. The talons of a hawk, provided with savage claws, not only grasp the prey but usually also deal the death-blow. The webbed feet of the ducks provide both an efficient paddle as a means of propulsion in water, and a load-spreading support when standing on soft mud. Other examples include the long, but unwebbed toes of the crake and wader families, again designed to support the birds on soft terrain; and the curious but powerful toes of the woodpeckers, arranged two forward and two back, which are well equipped for holding on to tree trunks.

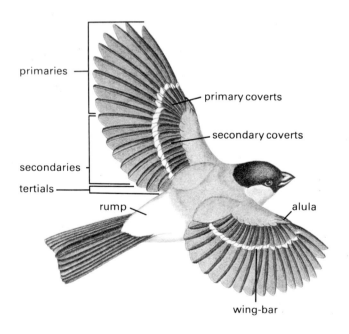

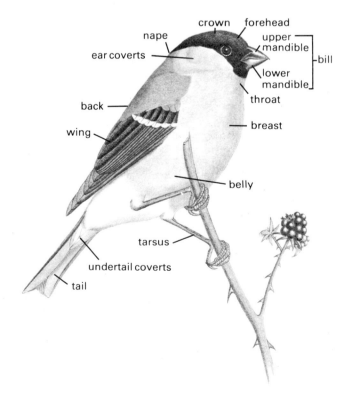

The complex structure of a bird's plumage is due to the fact that the body must maintain a streamlined, aerodynamic flight surface. The illustration also shows the major external features of birds described in this book.

## THE SKELETON

An examination of the skeleton of a bird reveals some remarkable features. One of the chief characteristics of bird bones is their lightness and strength. Although birds may have large bones, they are not massive in structure. Most are hollow, and some have large cavities which may contain extensions of the air sacs of the lungs. These long bones have occasional cross-struts, giving them extra strength and rigidity; this design is so sophisticated that it has been emulated by engineers in modern girder design. Bird bones are also many times lighter than a mammal bone of similar size.

The bird skeleton is basically a strong box: the vertebrae of the backbone are fused and joined to an elongate pelvis, or hip girdle. This axis is joined to the sternum, the keel-shaped breastbone, by a series of ribs, each of which has a small backward-

A bird bone in cross-section, showing the strengthening struts which give a rigid yet light structure.

pointing prong overlapping the rib behind. Within this box are safely situated most of the bird's organs. The centre of gravity of the compact body is close to the shoulder girdle, to which are attached the wings, and to the pelvis, where the legs are attached.

The legs and wings are composed of bones similar to those which form comparable limbs in mammals, although the proportions naturally differ. In the wing (or arm) of a bird, the upper arm (equivalent to our humerus) is short and strong; the forearm (equivalent to our radius and ulna) is long, and carries the feathers of the inner half of the wing which produce lift. The wrist and the hand are disproportionately large compared with man's, as it is here that the feathers which provide the propulsive power for flight are attached. A modification has also occurred in the legs: the thigh is short and stout, and the bones of the ankle and foot are much larger. What appears in the middle of a bird's leg as a 'back-to-front knee' is, in fact, its ankle!

The neck has a widely varying number of vertebrae: some species of swans may have 25, but house sparrows have only 16. Strangely, in all mammals the number is fixed at seven. The skull, together with the beak, are also essentially lightweight structures.

## BEAKS

The beak shows an amazing range of adaptations, almost all associated with the particular bird's feeding technique. Put simply, birds sacrificed hands, and manual dexterity, when they took to flight, and it is in the structural adaptations of their beaks that they achieve some compensation for this.

The range of beak types is huge, although the fundamental patterns are reasonably simple: a conical, wedge-shaped beak denotes a seed-crushing vegetarian life-style; short, finely pointed beaks suggest an insect eater; and hooked beaks are characteristic of flesh-tearing predators. There are also beaks for probing (like those of the waders); for stabbing (like the heron's); heavy-duty general-purpose beaks suiting omnivores such as the gull family; and the lighter omnivorous beaks of birds like song thrushes or blackbirds, which have a mixed diet of plant and animal material.

In many cases the shape of the beak alone is sufficiently diagnostic to identify the bird: the shoveler, avocet, crossbill and hawfinch all come to mind as examples of birds with characteristically shaped beaks. Perhaps the most striking of all is the 'upturned banana' beak of the flamingo. The flamingo feeds with its head upside-down near its feet, its beak immersed in water or sloppy mud. From this ooze it filters out small animals, collecting them on the whalebone-like edges of its beak. The flamingo's tongue lies in a depression in the beak, and it moves the tongue back and forth in an action similar to that of a bicycle pump, thus drawing food and water through the filters.

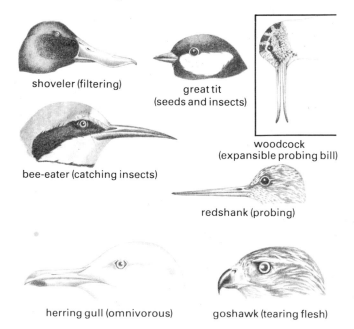

shoveler (filtering)

great tit (seeds and insects)

bee-eater (catching insects)

woodcock (expansible probing bill)

redshank (probing)

herring gull (omnivorous)

goshawk (tearing flesh)

A bird's beak is adapted to a particular feeding technique. Many birds can be identified by beaks alone.

# Breeding

Unlike mammals, birds have retained the ancestral reptilian egg both as the means of reproduction and as a protective capsule for the fertilized ovum as it develops through to hatching. Since this method of reproduction has endured already for over 100 million years, the egg must be considered as a success in evolutionary terms, but there can be no simple judgement as to whether bird reproduction, using eggs, is more efficient or satisfactory than the mammalian method in which a foetus develops inside its mother. Each has its advantages, and each has been tailored by adaptation and evolution to be the most effective method of reproduction for its particular purpose.

## EGG SIZE AND COLOUR

With the great range of bird sizes – from hummingbirds to ostriches – egg size variation is to be expected, but the relationship of body size to egg size is not a simple one since, broadly speaking, the smaller species lay proportionately larger eggs. For example, the blue tit egg weighs just over $\frac{1}{60}$ oz (0.5 g) – about 5 or 6 per cent of female body weight – whereas the ostrich egg, with a capacity approaching $\frac{1}{2}$ gallon (2.5 l), weighs about 50 oz (1400 g) – and that represents only 1 per cent of the female's total body weight.

In some cases the colours and patterns of eggs have a clear purpose. The eggs of the ringed plover, with blackish spots on a sandy-coloured background, are ideally camouflaged for the typical ringed plover nesting site of a sandy beach with flecks of dark seaweed and broken shell among the grains of sand. Hole-nesting birds, like owls and woodpeckers, lay whitish eggs, and it is thought that the pale colour may help the returning parents to locate the eggs in the sudden gloom as they enter the nest chamber from the bright daylight outside. In the crowded circumstances of nesting colonies, variations in shade and pattern may help the individual bird recognize its egg. This is particularly true in species like the guillemot, where an actual nest does not exist and the birds lay their single eggs side by side on sea cliff ledges. However, in other species – the tree pipit and the red-backed shrike are the most striking examples – the wide range of rich colours exhibited within each species is more difficult to explain.

## NESTING AND INCUBATION

The simplest nests are those in which the egg or eggs are laid directly on the ground. Any apparent risks in such a site due to predators may be reduced by physical factors – for instance the guillemot laying on exposed, but usually inaccessible cliff ledges, or by the concealment provided by the cryptic coloration of the eggs of certain species. Many wader nests appear superficially simple – just scrapes in the ground – but even these have a definite form and structure, and may even be ornamented with small pebbles, pieces of shell and flotsam and jetsam. The simple nest scrape is further developed by other waders, and by many ducks and gulls: dead vegetation and flotsam and jetsam is gathered into a mound with a depression at its centre containing the eggs.

Better physical protection is offered by the cup-shaped nest used by the majority of birds, particularly the small and medium-sized song birds. The eggs cluster naturally at the base of the cup, safe from physical disturbance and chilling by wind, and from the eyes of predators. Domed nests – such as the wren's – are extensions of the cup pattern offering a totally enclosed cavity to protect eggs and young. The flask-shaped nest of the long-tailed tit is composed of cobweb, hair, lichen and moss and has the additional advantage that it is flexible and can stretch, and can thus accommodate the brood as it grows up. Other tits, owls, the jackdaw and the stock dove seek the protection of the natural cavities in old trees, in cliff faces and in old buildings. The woodpeckers excavate their own nest holes in standing trees, and sand martins and kingfishers excavate nest burrows in suitable sandy soils.

In the tropics the pendant woven nests of the various species of weaver-birds demonstrate the most sophisticated pattern of nest building, but among European nesting species the mossy swinging hammock of the tiny goldcrest, or the basketwork nest of the reed warbler (incorporating a number of supporting reed stems and capable of withstanding gales and, quite regularly, the unwanted weight of a young cuckoo), are also fine examples of the art of nest building.

During the course of evolution a number of patterns of egg laying have emerged in various bird families, each evolved to be effective in particular circumstances. In Britain, the majority of blue and great tits depend on the caterpillars of the winter moth (which appear predominantly on oak trees) to feed their young. These caterpillars occur in enormous numbers, but for less than one month in early summer. To exploit this situation most blue and great tits are single-brooded, laying just one clutch of eggs, normally between eight and 15 in number, timed so that the young can be fed at the peak of caterpillar production. In contrast to this 'all eggs in one basket' approach, the majority of small and medium-sized song birds produce two or three clutches (sometimes more in a favourable summer), each of four to six eggs, allowing them to exploit a food supply which occurs at moderate levels throughout the summer, rather than in a single, short-lived glut. In both cases the food supply is effectively exploited. Larger birds may not have time, or available food supplies, to produce more than one or two eggs in a single clutch, or to raise the young successfully afterwards, so overall, food seems the dominant factor determining clutch size.

The incubation period – the time taken for the embryo to develop and hatch – varies considerably. Generally speaking, larger birds have longer incubation periods than smaller ones. Most song birds incubate their eggs for about two weeks, starting when the clutch is complete. As an adaptation to its parasitic life, cuckoo eggs hatch in only 11 or 12 days, giving the young cuckoo a chance to shoulder its foster parents' eggs out of the nest before they hatch. Ascending the size scale, gulls and ducks incubate for about three weeks; geese for about a month; the mute swan for 35 days; and, longest of all, the golden eagle and the gannet each incubate for about 45 days.

Often the female will do all, or most of, the incubation, leaving the nest only briefly to feed and drink. The belly sheds its down feathers to expose an oval patch of skin, wrinkled and richly supplied with blood vessels. It is the body heat transmitted by the blood in these vessels that incubates the eggs, and when a bird is settling down, with cautious shuffles, to begin brooding, it is to ensure that all the eggs are positioned beneath the brood-patch. Once the young have hatched, the male assumes more responsibility; particularly in the first few days of their life, when the female needs to remain at the nest to brood the nestlings for warmth and safety, he may carry the major burden of providing food for the whole family.

The drab winter plumage of the male golden plover provides camouflage and protection. In summer, however, the bird must attract a mate, and so it moults, revealing golden brown upperparts and a black-and-white face and breast pattern (inset).

# Migration

For birds as a whole, one of the major benefits of their powers of flight is that it enables them to travel to many parts of the earth to exploit food sources on a seasonal basis. Such movements, when carried out to a regular pattern, are called migrations, and they may be of several types. In Europe, we encounter the complete range.

Bird migration has been an accepted natural phenomenon since man first began to study birds, fascinating ancient civilizations as much as it intrigues us today. Over the centuries, as man has become more 'scientifically' interested in his surroundings, dispute has raged as to how the migrants navigated and where they went in winter. Even as recently as 300 years ago, swallows and martins were still thought by some to overwinter in the mud at the bottom of ponds!

Much work still needs to be done before we can understand fully the stimulus which causes migrant species to undertake what are often considerably hazardous and extremely long journeys. Experiments have shown that day length is an important factor, however, for it affects the hormone production of the pituitary gland, leading eventually to an overwhelming desire to embark upon migration. Among the effects of this hormonal activity are moulting and an increased level of feather maintenance, and the storage of energy in the form of fat, prior to the long flights ahead.

Many of the birds that breed in Europe during the summer months move away south to tropical Africa, or even further south, for the winter, to areas where their food (mainly composed of insects), is still in abundant supply. (In contrast, much of Europe has low temperatures in winter which greatly reduce the number of insects available as food.) Good examples of these migrants are the warbler family and the aerial-feeding species – swifts, swallows, martins and flycatchers.

Others, including some thrushes and many kinds of ducks and waders, operate a different pattern of food exploitation. They are able to survive the winter in western Europe – particularly the ducks and waders which overwinter in the slightly warmer regions close to the sea. They fly north and northwestward in spring, to areas which are snow-covered and inhospitable through the winter but which provide a rich food supply, mostly of insect life, at the onset of summer. During the perpetual daylight of the Arctic summer, the migrants exploit this food resource.

There is a third category, which is composed of birds breeding in the far north of Europe and migrating south, usually to Africa (or to the South Atlantic Ocean if they are seabirds). These are seen only as migrants in much of Europe, usually staying only briefly in April or May but making a more leisurely journey south during the autumn months.

It may be difficult to make a precise prediction about when a particular bird is likely to be seen on migration – and accuracy is made even more difficult by the varying influence of climate from year to year. Particularly severe winters will drive birds further south and west than usual, while particularly mild winter weather will allow even migrants to the tropics to remain well north of their usual wintering areas. At times of passage, the global weather pattern may influence the occurrence of rarities. In spring, some migrants normally resident only in southern Europe may 'overshoot' under the influence of a south-easterly tail wind, and may even stay on to breed. In autumn, powerful weather systems in the North Atlantic may bring American vagrants to western Europe on high-altitude jet-stream winds. Huge high-pressure areas over Europe and Asia, with gentle easterly winds, may bring numbers of oriental birds (like the tiny Pallas' warbler) far to the west of their normal haunts.

Most of the time birds migrate to and from their breeding grounds without attracting a great deal of attention, but there are nevertheless a few places where migration is so obvious that no one could fail to notice what is going on. An excellent example is the concentration of tens of thousands of birds of prey and storks crossing the narrow waters of the Bosphorus, on route between Europe and Asia and Africa. Another is the autumn gatherings of thousands of birds of prey at Falsterbo, in southern Sweden, prior to crossing the narrow straits separating Scandinavia from the main European land mass.

Inspired by the information that could be gathered in such circumstances, other early migration observation points were set up, manned by a few enthusiastic pioneers such as Eagle Clarke in the early years of this century. These were co-ordinated by no less a body than the British Association for the Advancement of Science, and

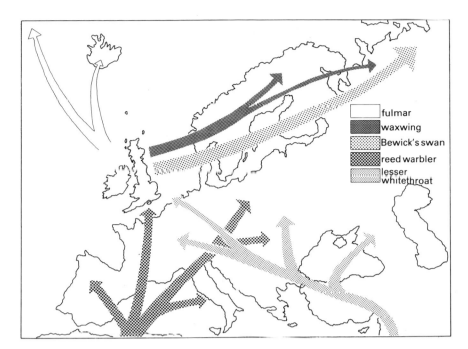

fulmar
waxwing
Bewick's swan
reed warbler
lesser whitethroat

The migration routes of some bird species. The reed warbler crosses the Mediterranean on a single front which fans out on the continent of Europe. By contrast, the lesser whitethroat migrates along two distinct routes: south in autumn through Greece, and north in spring through the Bosphorus.

tended to be situated on islands, headlands, isolated lighthouses and lightships that seemed to lie on natural north–south flyways. The modern bird observatories are located in very similar places, where it is relatively easy to monitor mass movements of birds.

The first proper bird observatory was founded by an enthusiastic amateur called Heinrich Gatke, who spent half a century on the island of Heligoland, off the German North Sea coast, in the latter part of the nineteenth century. Today, classical studies at observatories are augmented by radar observations. Radar has the great advantage that its use is unaffected by darkness, so that the massive nocturnal movements of many birds can be plotted. Regrettably, however, since it can only indicate size and numbers, it gives only the roughest idea of the bird's identity, so the birdwatcher cannot entirely be replaced by modern technology!

## RINGING

Ringing is the process of placing on a bird an individually numbered band, and is one of the ways in which migration is studied. Each ring has a return address stamped on it, to which the finder of a ringed dead bird is requested to send the ring. Ringing began at the end of the last century in Denmark, and two separate schemes began in Britain in 1909, merging in 1937. Now many European countries have organized schemes, with an international co-operative body called Euring which arranges for the use of standard techniques and forms. With automatic data processing facilities available, it is important that national records can be exchanged and processed elsewhere.

The first use of ringing was to determine the destinations and the routes taken by some of our migrants, and for many the route maps are now starting to fill up. For some, however, the picture is just beginning to become clear: the lesser white-throat, it appears, migrates southwards from Britain to the region of the Sudan in autumn via Italy and Egypt. Returning in spring, the route lies, it seems, further to the east, northwards through Israel and the Lebanon, before turning west, probably passing across Europe north of the Alps. This is called a loop migration.

More recently, ringing returns have also provided valuable information about birds' lifespans and causes of death.

Some of the really spectacular results so far produced concern the long-distance migration routes of some seabirds. Manx shearwaters breeding off western Europe winter off the coasts of Brazil, Argentina and Uruguay, and can manage the 6000 mile (9646 km) trip from their breeding islands in as little as a fortnight! Recently a British-ringed Manx shearwater was washed ashore in the Great Australian Bight. Kittiwakes and fulmars disperse widely across the Atlantic, while skuas, petrels and terns spread south of the equator. Northern European Arctic terns have been caught on whaling ships on the edge of the Antarctic pack-ice – an enormous distance to fly each migration season, and one which gives the birds almost continuous maximum day-length, as winter here is summer in the southern hemisphere. For sheer speed, a knot – an Arctic-breeding wader – ringed on southward autumn passage in eastern England and recovered in West Africa only eight days later, must take some beating.

# Birdwatching

Birdwatching is just one part of the whole subject of ornithology – the study of birds. Birdwatching is one of the fastest-growing pursuits and already attracts a tremendous following. It is also a flexible hobby. The amount of time devoted to it is under the control of the birdwatcher, although it must be admitted that (like many other pastimes) it *is* possible to get 'hooked' and find the hobby so compulsive that your spare time is spent doing little else.

The way in which birds are watched is again under the control of the individual: they can be simply looked at or identified; they can be admired, perhaps from a purely aesthetic angle; or they can be studied seriously. That study can vary from a life's work, often in inhospitable terrain, to the intimate watching of the comings and goings at a nestbox observed through the kitchen window.

Many birds have adapted so well to new habitats – particularly urban ones – that their sheer abundance means we do not need to travel far to see them. House sparrows, starlings, blackbirds and skylarks are good examples, as are those newest 'recruits', collared doves. Others must be sought out in their specialist habitats: such as bitterns with their preference for huge reed-beds, or the mountaintop ptarmigan. Seeking and finding these birds usually involves a special expedition, but with a special reward. There is a similar challenge in obtaining good views of the commoner and more widespread species like hawfinches, lesser spotted woodpeckers or grasshopper warblers, which have notoriously secretive habits.

## BINOCULARS AND TELESCOPES

It is perfectly possible to see and enjoy birds without any special equipment, but identification is simplified enormously by using a pair of binoculars. Distant birds cease to be tiny dots against water or sky and develop recognizable colours and shapes, and close-up views reveal that feathers have a beauty of their own. The use of binoculars also gives you the fascinating chance to spy on birds going about their daily lives undisturbed.

Because binoculars are the most important piece of birdwatching equipment, it is worth taking a great deal of care when you choose them. The first golden rule is to try them outdoors yourself. The magnification you will need depends on the sort of birdwatching which you will be doing, but remember that high-powered binoculars are often large and heavy. Additionally, the 'field of view' (the width of the image you see) usually becomes smaller with increasing magnification, so if you intend to watch birds mainly in woodland, choose a wide-angle pair of binoculars (a pair with a wide field of view) with lower magnification. High-magnification binoculars generally let in less light, so are less suitable for evening work, but are almost essential for watching on reservoirs and on the coast, where the birds are often very distant.

When you try your binoculars before buying, test them for comfort and balance. Do they fit well in your hands? Do the eyecups keep out any stray side-light? Do the focusing controls run smoothly at your fingertips? Check the quality of the image: it should appear natural in colour. A common fault with poorer binoculars is the appearance of a colour fringe which shows as a faint rainbow halo round the image. Also if you look at a vertical line, for example a telegraph pole, it should not appear to be bent, and your picture should be sharply in focus across the field of view (although a little less detail at the edges probably will not matter too much).

Expensive binoculars are not necessarily the best for birdwatching; there are now many excellent inexpensive binoculars on the market, so shop around. For long-distance work, and for the really serious birdwatcher on coasts, inland reservoirs and lakes, a telescope may be worthwhile. Although the magnification of telescopes (up to 50 times) is much greater than binoculars, using one eye can be tiring. The field of view of a telescope is tiny, which makes moving birds difficult to spot and the image is only really clear in bright sunshine. Also, telescopes are awkward and difficult to hold steady without a tripod. Modern telescopes, with variable-magnification eyepieces, are usually much easier to use than the long, old-fashioned brass spy-glass, however.

## BIRDWATCHING TECHNIQUES

Using binoculars is one way to bring the birds closer, but it is also possible to get much closer to the birds yourself. If wild creatures are not aware of a human presence they will continue to behave quite naturally, and perhaps pass quite close by. Unlike mammals, birds have no sense of smell, so there is no need to worry about the wind blowing your scent to them and frightening them. All birds have exceptionally keen eyesight, however, much better than human vision; a hovering kestrel is able to spot a beetle in the grass 130 ft (40 m) below! They also have acute hearing, and their ability to find food depends on the sharpness of these two senses.

So what does the birdwatcher need to do? First, always move about quietly: do not give the birds advance warning of your arrival or they will move away. Try the hunter's method of moving silently in woodland. Avoid crashing through the bushes, or snapping twigs and rotten branches underfoot. Pause often to listen. If the approach has been quiet, the various songs and calls will tell you which birds are nearby. Few people realize how helpful a good knowledge of birds songs and calls can be. Birds have a whole series of calls, ranging from the 'Here I am' call that helps to keep a flock together, to a 'Come-for-food' call. Alarm notes are usually short and strident. Parent birds have special calls that they use to signal to their young, including a different, much softer, danger signal that means 'Keep quiet and still, there is danger about'. Once bird calls and songs can be recognized, you will know which species of birds to expect and will have a better chance of seeing them.

When starting birdwatching, it is always best to note down details of the birds seen, with sketches if possible. Pay particular attention to their size compared with other birds that you know, as well as their general shape and 'deportment'. Striking features such as the beak, legs, feet and plumage are worth noting also. The same applies even for the skilled birdwatcher confronted with an unknown bird, and as the fieldguides and textbooks use the same terms to identify various parts of the body (see page 8), it is well worth while becoming familiar with them.

Thus, in time, your notebook will become filled with details. Some may refer to plumage colours, beak shapes and sizes, but the more useful, and essentially personal, ones should refer to *your* interpretation of calls and songs. The other valuable element is popularly called 'jizz'. This useful term embraces all those complex features such as wing shape, how the bird stands, runs (or hops), walks and flies, and what features stand out at a distance; in essence how *you* know — almost instinctively when you become more experienced — what bird it is that you are looking at.

Always walk slowly in good birdwatching country. Use the natural cover provided by banks, trees and bushes. Before you reach a gap, pause and listen for a few moments, then look around.

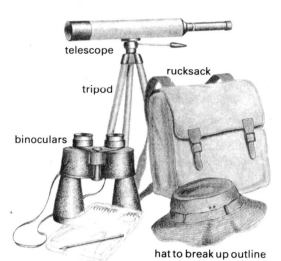

Basic birdwatching equipment. Binoculars are an essential item, but the telescope and tripod are only needed for sea and estuary watching. A strong rucksack is useful for carrying all your equipment.

Sometimes stand still for a while, and let the bird betray its presence by moving before you do. Do your best to avoid sudden movements. Avoid wearing brightly coloured clothes, but choose instead dark blue which is probably the least conspicuous, and try not to wear stiff materials that will crackle or scrape on twigs and leaves.

Having obtained a good view of the bird the task now is to identify it. Most birdwatchers find the number of birds illustrated in a fieldguide bewildering. This is partly because there are so many species, arranged in what may appear to be quite a random manner, and partly because most guides cover areas as large as a continent, and will include many birds that the 'average' birdwatcher is unlikely to encounter. However, even in those guides in which the birds appear to be randomly grouped there is normally a pattern. Most usually the birds are arranged in families, beginning with the divers and finishing with the passerines, or perching birds. This is known as taxonomic order. The drawback with this method is that if you see a bird you wish to identify, you may have to search through several pages of similar species (which do not even appear in the habitat in which you saw your bird) before you find the right one.

Another approach, and the one used in this book, groups the birds under relatively broad habitat headings. In this way, the birds seen on a visit to an estuary, a wood or reed-bed, for instance, are grouped together and come readily to hand rather than being scattered through the pages of the fieldguide. Unfortunately, even this apparently commonsense approach is not foolproof; because birds are so mobile they may be seen in several different habitats, especially at different times of the year. A tired migrant may be seen just about anywhere and occasional storm-driven ocean birds will turn up on inland reservoirs. Furthermore, the most opportunist species, like the blue tit, will occur in winter stealing the cream from doorstep milk bottles, seeking hibernating insects in reed-beds, as well as in the woods, farms and gardens which are their accustomed habitats.

## HOW TO USE THIS BOOK

The majority of European species you are likely to encounter frequently, some 250 in all, are included and illustrated in this book. The birds are described according to their habitats, and these have been divided into six groups: birds of mountain and moorland; heath and maquis; woodland; downland and man-made habitats; wetlands; and coasts and estuaries. Each of these habitats is described in detail with the aid of full-colour illustrations depicting typical views with representative species of birds. All the most commonly encountered birds in each habitat are then described, together with plumage details, breeding behaviour and distribution. The map opposite will help you to check whether or not a particular bird occurs in your area. Other points of general interest are also given, in particular any 'field signs' which will help you to positively identify the bird. Each species is depicted by means of a colour photograph and a field guide illustration – the latter have been carefully selected to show off the identification features of the birds.

This book can be used in two quite separate ways. If you were planning a trip to, say, the coast, then a quick glance through the chapter describing the birds of coastal habitats would give you a good idea of what to look out for when you arrive. Part of the trick of successful bird identification is knowing which birds are likely to be present in a particular habitat. Alternatively the book can be used as a straightforward identification guide, or just to provide you with some interesting facts about a bird you may have already identified.

A few terms used in the text may need clarification. A bird described as a **summer visitor** to a region breeds there and migrates in the autumn to a wintering area, returning again to the breeding region the following spring. Thus swallows are summer visitors to Britain and northern Europe and spend our European winter in South Africa. A **resident** bird remains in a given area throughout the year. **Eclipse plumage** is the dull plumage which male ducks in particular may be seen in after their breeding season. Key: ♂ denotes male; ♀ denotes female.

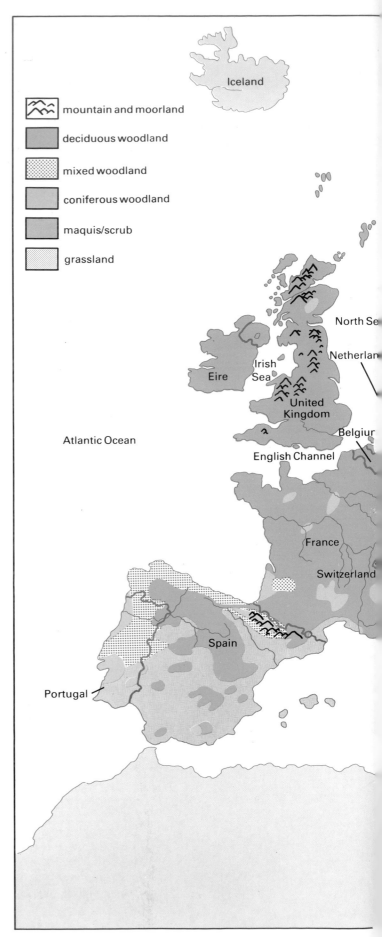

mountain and moorland

deciduous woodland

mixed woodland

coniferous woodland

maquis/scrub

grassland

Iceland

North Se

Netherlan

Irish
Sea

Eire

United
Kingdom

Belgiur

Atlantic Ocean

English Channel

France

Switzerland

Spain

Portugal

Barents Sea

Norwegian Sea

Finland

USSR

Sweden

Norway

Denmark

Baltic Sea

West Germany

East Germany

Poland

Czechoslovakia

Austria

Hungary

Romania

Black Sea

Yugoslavia

Italy

Adriatic Sea

Bulgaria

Albania

Aegean Sea

Turkey

Greece

Mediterranean Sea

This map shows the main natural vegetation zones of Europe. The impact of man has, however, often resulted in a diverse patchwork of landscapes within these major zones. Thus, for instance, farmland, heathland and cities – man's own environment – have all become established habitats in their own right.

# Mountain and moorland

Mountain and moorland provide perhaps the most visually dramatic of all the European bird habitats. In many of these upland regions, however, the purple and golden tints of summer are replaced by the harsh, snow-covered waste of winter, making survival a constant struggle.

Mountain and moorland are among the remotest and most ancient of the natural habitats for birds and, superficially at least, seem to be the least vulnerable to change, or indeed to actual damage, at the hand of man. When the history of moorland and the present-day recreational use of mountains are considered, however, ample contrasts can be found to this apparent stability.

The mountains of Britain and Ireland are about 3200 ft (1000 m) high, and those of the Alps reach a height of 13,000 ft (4000 m). All these mountainous regions have many features in common, however. Part of the reason for this lies in their formation: mountains arose in the distant geological past as a result of violent movements in the earth's crust. These movements caused the crust to bulge.

The fate of the 'bulge' depends on a number of factors, the most important of which are the age and nature of the rocks. The Alps, for example, are comparatively young, and have not been subjected to long periods of weathering. As a consequence, they remain jagged, high peaks, whereas the older mountains of northern and western Britain and Ireland have, over millions of years, worn down to give them their familiar 'round-shouldered' appearance. The nature of the rock is also important: the softer limestones erode and weather far more quickly than the harder granites, though in time, even these weather.

There is a vast difference in appearance between the mountains, with their majestic peaks and plunging ravines, and moors, which are often flat or only gently rolling. Moorland is the buffer zone between man-managed farmland and the moun-tains, but fingers of moorland penetrate around the foothills and often well into mountain ranges. Although it does not usually exhibit such severe conditions as mountains, moorland does nevertheless occupy high ground and is often harsh enough to exclude many of the farm or forest birds.

Most moorland lies in areas of high rainfall, and is normally damp. The soil is an impermeable clay topped with a deep layer of peat, which is itself the part-decayed residue of moss and heather. Bogs are commonplace in the hollows; these are perpetually wet areas, usually with a plant community very limited by the acidic and oligotrophic nature of the water and soil, which effectively prevent the growth of a richer, more diverse plant community.

Despite the natural appearance of the scenery, it is rarely appreciated that many areas of moorland are comparatively recent, created by man within the last few centuries. Good evidence of this is to be found in the part-fossilized tree stumps so common on moors: these are the tangible remains of woodland which was cleared to make way for more grassland, and thus provide grazing for livestock. Now, in remote areas, the peat that developed on the soils so suddenly exposed to climatic extremes and erosion is itself under attack. Once dug by man and dried for fuel, more and more is being extracted to refurbish exhausted garden soils.

Neither is the ecology of the mountains safe from the hands of man. At these high altitudes such plants as do occur are highly specialized, and plant growth is very slow. Thus damage due to overgrazing by, say, herbivores like red deer (encouraged to flourish as game for subsequent shooting) or reindeer (introduced as an additional tourist attraction) can be disastrous. On the high tops, vehicle tracks made over the alpine vegetation may cause such damage that the habitat requires decades to recover. In the worst cases, plant destruction is promptly followed by soil erosion.

Such, though, has been the increase in hill walking, rock climbing and skiing that access roads, cable cars and chair lifts are becoming increasingly profitable investments and thus increasingly widespread. Because of them, greatly increased numbers of people can be conveyed quickly to this very sensitive area. So now, paradoxically, the major threat facing the mountain ecosystem comes from people eager to see and enjoy it.

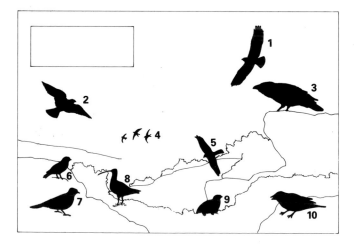

1 golden eagle
(*Aquila chrysaetos*)
2 peregrine (*Falco peregrinus*)
3 raven (*Corvus corax*)
4 alpine swift (*Apus melba*)
5 hen harrier (*Circus cyaneus*)
6 black redstart
(*Phoenicurus ochruros*)
7 blue rock thrush
(*Monticola solitarius*)
8 curlew (*Numenius arquata*)
9 ptarmigan (*Lagopus mutus*)
10 ring ouzel (*Turdus torquatus*)

## BIRDS OF MOUNTAIN AND MOORLAND

It is on the high tops that the mountain specialists are encountered. The peregrine, a large and more powerfully built relative of the merlin, is best known for its prowess as a hunter. Peregrines often patrol high in the sky, waiting like old-fashioned fighter

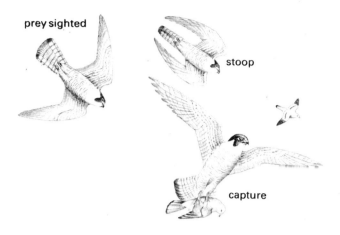

prey sighted

stoop

capture

A peregrine pursues its quarry.

planes for prey to pass beneath. Then they descend, at speeds well in excess of 60 mph (100 kph), striking their prey with outstretched talons and knocking it lifeless in mid-air.

Having endured threats to their continued existence from gamekeepers, egg collectors and poisonous chemicals in insecticides, peregrines are now threatened by their own popularity as birds to be trained for the ancient sport of falconry, and many young are stolen from their eyries each year.

The golden eagle is another predator of the mountainsides. They also nest on crags (occasionally in trees), in ancestral sites that may have been used by successive pairs of eagles for more than a century. Feeding by scavenging and eating carrion as much as by hunting, golden eagles need a vast territory to support them year-round, and a single pair may sometimes patrol 40 square miles (103 km²) or more. Majestic and powerful when soaring on their huge broad wings, golden eagles are remarkably agile and aerobatic when stooping suddenly at prey such as a mountain hare, startled into fleeing as the eagle swoops across the flank of the hill.

Even the boulder-strewn mountain summits support certain species of birds. One, the sparrow-sized snow bunting, is a summer visitor only, eking out a living from seeds and insects; but the other, the ptarmigan, is a genuine high-altitude specialist. Ptarmigan are year-round birds of these exposed areas, their plumage magnificent camouflage against the lichens in summer and the snow in winter. With feet feathered down to the toes as insulation, ptarmigan avoid the worst of the weather by tunnelling beneath the snows. Here, as in an igloo, the snow provides insulation and warmth, and there is plenty of greenstuff in the form of heather shoots for food.

This is harsh terrain for man as well as for birds. More than in any other habitat, birdwatching here

calls for forethought and planning. Despite modern communications and modern road networks, much of the best birdwatching may be found away from the beaten track and at a distance from vehicle access. Thus mountain and moorland birdwatchers should be well prepared for a long and often arduous walk. The climate is fickle in the extreme and can change almost in an instant, so even in midsummer, warm and waterproof clothing is an essential. Ample food and drink must be carried, as fog or low cloud can quickly blanket the area, making getting lost all too easy. Carry a map, whistle and compass, and inform others of your route and your expected time of return before you set out.

Even moorland is harsh terrain, particularly during the winter. Relatively few small birds find its windblown and often wet expanses an acceptable habitat, but meadow pipits and the almost ubiquitous skylarks are among the few that do, with other species like the whinchat breeding near the boundary between true moorland and rough upland grass land. The meadow pipit is perhaps *the* characteristic small bird of all types of moorland. In fine spring weather it can be seen indulging in parachuting display song-flights, and in less favourable conditions scampering about feeding on the ground. Even for meadow pipits and skylarks the moorland expanses may be too bleak in winter, and many will descend to lower altitudes or migrate south for the winter.

Meadow pipits are common foster-parents or hosts to cuckoos; they are medium-sized moorland birds, easily finding enough caterpillars in the summer to survive, as a number of moths flourish on the moorland vegetation. Where the moor is split by a ravine with a tumbling stream, or punctuated by an isolated rowan tree, then there is a chance of a ring ouzel territory. Appropriately also called 'mountain blackbirds', ring ouzels penetrate as a summer visitor almost to the high tops of the mountains, often nesting on the ground, even occasionally beneath it in an old mineshaft. Ring ouzels have a simple but powerful and melodic song, certainly one that embellishes the moorland spring.

If any song is evocative of the moorland atmosphere, it must be the bubbling, trilling exulting torrent of notes of the curlew. Of the larger moorland birds, this is surely the most tuneful. The wader family has three widespread moorland breeding representatives: the curlew, golden plover and diminutive dunlin, joined in the farthest north by the whimbrel. All are summer visitors only to the moors, as normally is the merlin, a small low-flying falcon. Merlins often subsist largely on the ever-present meadow pipits, but will, if opportunity arises, tackle birds as big as ring ouzels and dunlins.

◄ **GOLDEN EAGLE** *Aquila chrysaetos*
**Length** 33 in (83 cm).
**Appearance** Huge, with long, broad, fingered wings. Adults tawny brown, with golden tinge on nape of neck. Immatures have much white in the tail and wings.
**Distribution** Resident in north and north-east Europe (including Britain) and Spain, and countries bordering the Mediterranean.

The commonest and most widespread of the western European eagles, with a flourishing stronghold in Scotland. Such large birds, partly dependent on carrion, partly on prey such as grouse, ptarmigan and mountain hares – caught by surprise after a thrilling swoop close above the mountainside – require a large territory. These are often tens of square miles in extent, and so sightings are inevitably few and far between. Sadly, golden eagles are still the target of trapping, shooting and poisoning, in the mistaken belief that their presence disrupts grouse shoots and deer stalking, and that they regularly carry off lambs. They lay two (occasionally three) white eggs flecked with brown, in a single clutch.

**ROUGH-LEGGED BUZZARD►**
*Buteo lagopus*
**Length** 23 in (58 cm).
**Appearance** Pale streaky brown above – usually darker brown on belly, but plumage varies considerably; underwing pale, with dark blob on midwing; tail white with broad black terminal bar.
**Distribution** Breeds in far north of Europe; winters in central and eastern Europe, and eastern parts of Britain.

Although common in barren, mountainous country across northern Europe, rough-legged buzzards are scarce autumn and winter visitors to Britain, usually occurring on wide, sparsely populated areas of coastal marshland. This difference in habitat preference, and the rough-legged buzzards' habit of hovering (like a huge, but less rigid kestrel) help to distinguish them from the common buzzard (*B. buteo*). Their occurrence in Britain is erratic: some years only a few birds may be seen, in widely scattered localities, while in others several birds may be seen hunting over the same marsh. There is one clutch, containing up to four white eggs with red-brown blotches and streaks.

**HEN HARRIER** *Circus cyaneus* ▲
**Length** 19 in (48 cm).
**Appearance** Adult males pale grey above, with white rump; wing-tips black; underparts white; conspicuous white rump above long barred tail. Females and immatures brown above, buff-streaked brown below.
**Distribution** Breeds in north and north-east Europe (including Britain), also resident in some areas; winters in west and south-west Europe.

Unlike the other two harriers – the marsh (*C. aeruginosus*) and Montagu's (*C. pygargus*) – which are summer visitors, hen harriers are resident in many areas. Their habit of flying low on out-stretched wings, with only the occasional flap, as they quarter the ground regularly in search of prey, is a useful aid to identification. In the summer, breeding pairs can be found on northern moorlands and they increasingly exploit successfully the growing acreage of young conifer plantations. Up to six bluish-white eggs are laid. Numbers are larger in winter due to an influx of migrants from further north and east. Coastal and freshwater marshes are the usual winter habitat, although odd birds may be seen almost anywhere inland.

## MONTAGU'S HARRIER *Circus pygargus* ▶
**Length** 16 in (40 cm).
**Appearance** Adult males grey above, paler below, wings grey with black tips and a black bar on the inner half. Females brown, paler but streaked below, with small white rump-patch. Young resemble females but are more chestnut and less streaked.
**Distribution** Widespread summer visitor to most of Europe (including a few in England and Wales). In spring and autumn, numbers in western Europe are augmented by migrants from further east.

Montagu's harriers exploit a wide range of habitats, including farmland, moorland, young forestry plantations, sand dunes and marshes. Like other harriers, they catch their prey (which includes worms, frogs, lizards, snakes, small mammals and birds) by taking it by surprise, gliding low over the ground before making a sudden pounce. Up to five off-white eggs are laid.

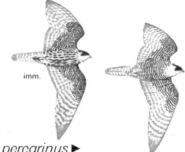

imm.

## PEREGRINE *Falco peregrinus* ▶
**Length** 16–20 in (40–50 cm).
**Appearance** Adults grey above; dark moustachial stripes contrasting with pale throat and cheeks; white below, finely barred black. Females appreciably larger than males. Young birds browner, with heavily streaked buffish underparts.
**Distribution** Breeds in most of north and north-east Europe (including Britain); winters over most of Europe.

The largest and most spectacular of the British and Irish falcons – although several other European falcons are considerably larger – peregrines breed among the hills and mountains of the north and west, usually on an inaccessible rocky ledge and occasionally in a disused raven's nest. Up to five, usually dark red eggs are laid. In winter, some birds move south and join others of Continental origin on extensive areas of coastal marshes. Peregrines hunt by circling at high altitude, waiting for suitable prey to pass. This they capture after a thrilling high-speed dive or stoop, the victim often being killed outright by the force of the mid-air impact.

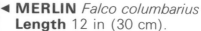
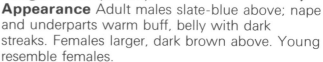

◄ **MERLIN** *Falco columbarius*
**Length** 12 in (30 cm).
**Appearance** Adult males slate-blue above; nape and underparts warm buff, belly with dark streaks. Females larger, dark brown above. Young resemble females.
**Distribution** Breeds in north and north-west Europe; winters in central and southern Europe; resident in northern and western Britain.

In the breeding season, merlins are birds of moorland, hill country and remote coastal areas. Up to five eggs are laid, which are densely speckled purplish-brown. In winter, most descend to the lowlands and many move south-east to large expanses of coastal marshes. Often to be seen perching in wait, merlins secure their prey (usually small birds) by a swift, low-level pursuit, culminating in a short climb taking them above their intended victim before the final strike.

◄ **PTARMIGAN** *Lagopus mutus*
**Length** 14 in (35 cm).
**Appearance** Winter plumage pure white except for black tail. In summer, wings and underparts remain white and rest of body is finely mottled yellow-brown; legs and feet feathered, white.
**Distribution** Resident in Britain and northern Europe.

With their plumages ideally adapted to mountain-top life by providing good camouflage in both winter and summer, ptarmigan are one of the few birds able to endure the winter at, and above, 2000 ft (650 m). Their feathered feet provide insulation against the chill from snow and ice, and in the depths of winter they find food by tunnelling beneath the snow to reach the heather, gaining an igloo-like shelter at the same time. On the Continent of Europe, the similar but reddish-brown and white willow grouse (*L. lagopus*) occurs on moorland at lower altitudes, but in Britain and Ireland the moorland bird is the completely russet-brown red grouse (*L. lagopus scoticus*), famous as the target game bird for sportsmen on August 12th. Five to nine eggs are produced; these are pale, but densely speckled with reddish chocolate colours and are laid in a shallow scrape.

## BLACK GROUSE ►
*Lyrurus tetrix*
**Length** 20 in (50 cm).
**Appearance** Males unmistakeable with iridescent blue-black plumage and long black tail with the outer feathers in the shape of a lyre contrasting sharply with white undertail feathers; white wing-bar conspicuous on rounded wings in flight. Females and young short-tailed and with duller plumage, speckled grey and brown for camouflage.
**Distribution** Resident in north and north-east Europe (including Britain).

For much of the year, black grouse are gregarious birds of moorland/woodland margins. The most fascinating aspect of their social life is the 'lekking' behaviour of the adult males or blackcock, which persists at varying intensities throughout the year. The males gather at an open area, the lek – a traditional patch of short grass which may have been in use for decades – and display their prowess in a series of mock battles with their fellows, against a background of extraordinary crowing, bubbling and hissing calls. Females, or greyhens, from the flocks of hens and young males visit the lek and select a mate. After mating, the greyhen moves off on her own to build a nest, usually in a shallow depression in the ground hidden by a tussock, and away from others of her kind for safety. Up to ten yellowish eggs with red-brown spots are laid in a single clutch.

## CURLEW ►
*Numenius arquata*
**Length** 23 in (58 cm).
**Appearance** Unmistakeable; adults and young sandy buff above, flecked and streaked with brown, paler below shading to white on belly; beak long – 5 in (13 cm) – and down-curved.
**Distribution** Breeds in north and north-east Europe (including Britain); winters in west and south-west.

During the summer months, curlews are moorland breeding birds; their song – a cascading, fluting babble – is produced by the male as he glides

parachute-like down to the ground after a swift upward climb. Usually four green-olive eggs with dark spots are laid. During the winter months, curlews are birds of coasts and estuaries with extensive mud or sandflats, where their long beak is used to good advantage to obtain worms and shellfish burrowing beyond the reach of other waders. At this time the call is a soulful 'coor-lee' after which the bird is named.

## WHIMBREL ▲
*Numenius phaeopus*
**Length** 16 in (40 cm).
**Appearance** Adults and young grey-brown, flecked with white above; buff below with darker streaks, paling to white on belly; three conspicuous buff bars on dark crown; beak long and down-curved.

**Distribution** Breeds in north and north-east Europe (including parts of Britain); winters in west and south-west.

In the breeding season, in which four olive-green eggs with dark spots are laid, whimbrel are scarce and confined to moorland and tundra areas in extreme northern Europe, penetrating as far south as the northern and western isles of Scotland. Elsewhere they are regularly seen along coasts and in estuaries on spring and autumn passage between their Arctic breeding grounds and African winter quarters. In flight they have a characteristic clear whistling repetitive call, which has earned them the colloquial name 'seven whistler'.

28

**SHORT-EARED OWL** ▶
*Asio flammeus*
**Length** 15 in (38 cm).
**Appearance** Sandy-brown, above, paler below,
heavily mottled with darker brown and little white
in wings; dark patch visible in flight at 'wrist' of
pale underside to wing; inconspicuous 'ear' tufts.
**Distribution** Summer visitor to north; resident
central and west Europe (including northern
Britain); winter visitor to south.

Short-eared owls are residents of open areas of
grass, scrub, moor and marsh. They are widely
distributed but never numerous. As with the other
owls, their breeding cycle is closely linked to food
supply: in years when voles are plentiful, double-
brooded pairs are common, and clutches may reach
11 eggs. In years of scarcity, they may lay just one or
two eggs, or none at all. The average is about seven
eggs. As an additional safety factor, owl eggs are
laid at intervals – usually every two days –
incubation beginning with the first. Thus the chicks
have staggered hatching times and vary considerably in size: if food shortage threatens, the
largest has at least one available food source – its
younger brothers or sisters.

**ALPINE SWIFT** *Apus melba* ▶
**Length** 8 in (20 cm).
**Appearance** Grey-brown above, with long,
sickle-shaped wings and shallowly forked tail;
white below, with brown breast-band and
brownish flanks.
**Distribution** Summer visitor to the southern
parts of Europe.

Alpine swifts are common in rocky mountain gorges
and in many towns and cities around the
Mediterranean, where their loud trilling song
contrasts with the screams of the common swift (*A.
apus*). Although they have the typical swift
silhouette, their brown-and-white plumage and
sheer size help to easily distinguish them from the
swift. Alpine swifts are scarce vagrants to Britain
and Ireland, usually occurring in spring or autumn.
There is one clutch annually, usually with three, or
four, dull white eggs.

**RAVEN** *Corvus corax* ▶
**Length** 25 in (63 cm).
**Appearance** All black, with broad heavily 'fingered' wings; heavy head with massive beak and bristling throat feathers; wedge-shaped tail.
**Distribution** Resident in most parts of Britain and Europe, except central Europe.

Although they were once common across the lowlands, persecution by gamekeepers and shepherds over the last two centuries has driven ravens high into the hills and to rocky and remote coastlines where they may breed unmolested. Ravens have a thrilling, tumbling aerobatic display, the male and female grasping each others' talons and plunging towards the ground, their harsh croaks echoing off the crags and cliffs. Ravens breed early, and even high in the hills, females may be sitting on eggs during February blizzards. Up to six eggs are laid, and these are pale blue-green with brown spots.

**CHOUGH** *Pyrrhocorax pyrrhocorax* ▶
**Length** 15 in (38 cm).
**Appearance** Adults glossy black all over, with slender down-curved crimson beak and crimson legs and feet. Young birds browner, with yellow beak and brown legs.
**Distribution** Resident in west and south-west Europe, and Britain.

Now very much restricted to the west coastal cliffs in the north and west, and to mountain areas in central and southern Europe, choughs are noisy birds, their loud, ringing 'kee-ow' calls resounding above the noise of the waves. They have rounded, 'fingered' wings, and delight in swooping and tumbling aerobatics in the strong upcurrents of air at the cliff face. Choughs nest, often colonially, in sea caves, laying up to five whitish eggs, mottled with brown and grey in a single clutch. They spend much of their feeding time seeking ants and similar insects along the cliff-top where the turf is short, or feeding on worms in freshly ploughed fields.

**RING OUZEL** ▶▶
*Turdus torquatus*
**Length** 10 in (25 cm).
**Appearance** Adult males sooty-black, with bold white crescent-shaped bib. Females brown, more speckled, bib often less distinct. Young scaly-brown, lacking bib.
**Distribution** Summer visitor to the uplands of northern, western and southern Europe (including Britain).

Ring ouzels are often appropriately called 'mountain blackbirds'. In Britain they are found mostly in the north and west of England and Wales, and in Scotland, but they are not as widespread as would be expected in Ireland. Ring ouzels replace blackbirds when trees become few and far between, only nesting at low altitudes in the extreme north. Most nests are on the ground, on ledges in rocky gullies, and a few are below ground level in caves or disused mine shafts. The highest nests may be found at well over 3000 ft (914 m). Up to six eggs are laid, which are blue-green with reddish blotches and there are often two broods.

# BLUE ROCK THRUSH *Monticola solitarius* ▶
**Length** 8 in (20 cm).
**Appearance** Adult males unmistakeable, slate-blue head and body; black wings and tail. Females and young are brownish-grey, and heavily flecked with buff.
**Distribution** Resident in southern Europe.

Unlike the rock thrush (*M. saxatilis*), blue rock thrushes are residents of rocky and hilly areas surrounding the Mediterranean, preferring habitats with more vegetation and at lower altitudes than their relative. They are shy birds, usually diving for cover among the rocks if disturbed, but have a loud thrush-like song which is both musical and evocative of their habitat. They are very scarce vagrants north of their range. Up to six eggs are laid, in two broods, and these are blue-green with sparse brown spots.

## BLACK REDSTART ▶
*Phoenicurus ochruros*
**Length** 6 in (15 cm).
**Appearance** Adult males ash-grey above, sooty-black below paling to a white belly; wings black with white patch; tail rich chestnut. Female and young have the chestnut tail but are otherwise sombre grey-brown.
**Distribution** Resident in south-west, western and southern Europe; summer visitor to north-east Europe (including Britain).

Black redstarts are widespread on the Continent in habitats as diverse as mountainside screes and the tiled rooftops of towns. In Britain their history is strange. In the 1930s they were scarce passage migrants, until a few pairs bred. The Second World War created, as an aftermath of the otherwise terrible blitz, expanses of scree-like rubble in the hearts of some southern cities, and here black redstarts settled and flourished as breeding birds. The population is still small and largely confined to the same area, often nesting on massive buildings such as power stations. Usually four to six white eggs are laid, sometimes faintly spotted. There are two broods.

## TWITE *Acanthis flavirostris* ▼
**Length** 5 in (13 cm).
**Appearance** Streaked dull brown above, paler below, shading to white on belly; beak yellow in winter, dark in summer. Males in summer have pink patch on otherwise pale rump.
**Distribution** Resident (and winter visitor) to northern Britain and north and north-west Europe.

Twite are often called 'mountain linnets', a name which is reflected in their breeding season distribution, which over much of northern Europe centres on upland areas and mountain chains. In the north and west, particularly near the coast, twite may breed at quite low altitudes. In winter, twite frequent open land with plentiful weed seed supplies, tending to congregate in flocks (sometimes hundreds strong) on coastal marshes, where they may feed among tide-line flotsam. The eggs are dark blue and heavily marked and a normal clutch size is six. Sometimes there are two broods.

**ROCK BUNTING** *Emberiza cia* ▶
**Length** 6 in (15 cm).
**Appearance** Males streaked brown above; grey head with striking pattern of black lines; underparts cinnamon. Females and young duller and browner, but with the same head pattern as adult.
**Distribution** Resident in southern Europe.

Extremely scarce vagrants to Britain and Ireland, rock buntings are fairly common in mountainous terrain in southern Europe, nesting in a broad belt extending from cultivated areas such as vineyards and olive groves in rocky valleys upwards until only scattered bushes remain. Birds living at high altitudes move to lower ground to escape the severity of winter. Up to six pale blue eggs with fine purple-brown squiggles are laid.

**SNOW BUNTING** *Plectrophenax nivalis* ▶
**Length** 6 in (15 cm).
**Appearance** Summer males white, with black back, wings and centre to tail. Females, young, and winter males mottled ginger-brown above, white below, large white patches on wings.
**Distribution** Summer visitor to the far north of Europe; winters in Britain and northern Europe.

Snow buntings breed on the hill tops and tundra along the northern coasts of Europe, but a few pairs nest each year on the tops of the highest mountains in the Cairngorms in the Highlands of Scotland, laying four to six eggs with reddish spots. In winter, these and other birds from further north move south to the lowlands. During these months snow buntings are typical of weedy pastures and stubble close to the sea — particularly of the band of

vegetation left by the tide on sandy or shingly beaches. Here, snow buntings as they feed are surprisingly inconscpicuous until put to flight, when their bold white markings make them easy to identify.

# Heathland and maquis

The dry, sandy heaths of Britain and Europe – already few and far
between – are under constant threat from land reclamation schemes.
Inevitably they, and the hilly thorn scrub of the Mediterranean basin
known as maquis, provide homes for some of the most interesting
and unusual species of birds.

## HEATHLAND AND ITS BIRDS

Over much of northern Europe heathland is a scarce habitat. Partly because of its scarcity, and partly because the soils on which heaths occur (which are easily worked), heathland is perhaps under greater threat than any other habitat. Much of the threat comes from attempts to reclaim heathland and turn it to a variety of agricultural uses. Most heaths are characterized by light sandy soils – usually acidic in nature – and by their vegetation, in which various heathers, gorse and stunted pines dominate a range of smaller acid-loving flowering plants and grasses.

Most heaths occur in relatively low-rainfall areas, and the dryness of the vegetation is tempting to those who feel that burning off the gorse and heather will improve the growth of grass so that the heath can be used for grazing stock. Equally, as the soils are light and thus usually easily worked, the temptation is ever-present to plough this so-called marginal land and convert it to productive agricultural use. Sadly, although a great deal of such reclamation has been carried out – in the process utterly destroying the nature of the heathland or so fragmenting its distribution as to make the isolated pockets almost worthless ecologically – there is little evidence in the majority of cases that agriculturally it has been worthwhile. That this is a difficult, impoverished soil, with related water problems, is amply borne out by the specialist nature of the natural vegetation it supports. It would be difficult, and very costly, to remedy this.

A number of birds typical of farmland hedges and scrub also adapt readily to heathland: species like

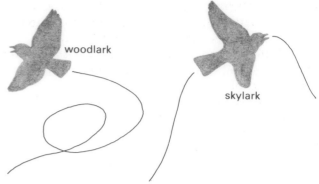

The skylark and the woodlark have distinctive song flights. The skylark soars upwards on fluttering wings, whereas the woodlark flies in a circle, often from a song-post.

the yellowhammer and linnet, often to be seen atop a gorse bush blazing with colour, or the less-conspicuous whitethroat and dunnock. Open landscape birds like skylarks and meadow pipits are at home on heaths, too, as is the curlew in the breeding season, which may nest in any of the damper areas caused by the drainage being impeded. (Presumably both curlew and meadow pipit find habitat similarities with their more normal moorland breeding areas.)

There are, however, more typical species, of which the robin-like stonechat is perhaps the most noisily conspicuous; its 'chack' call is reminiscent of pebbles being struck together. Stonechats, though alert and noisy, are not frightened by intruders, and give the birdwatcher excellent views as they accompany him closely – always perching on bush tops with wings flicking and tail cocked – as he passes through their territory. In some areas the dark and skulking Dartford warbler occurs, and in others nightjars are to be found. Nightjars are

1 nightjar
   (*Caprimulgus europaeus*)
2 stonechat (*Saxicola torquata*)
3 hobby (*Falco subbuteo*)
4 black-eared wheatear
   (*Oenanthe hispanica*)
5 stone curlew
   (*Burhinus oedicnemus*)
6 bee-eater (*Merops apiaster*)

7 red-legged partridge
   (*Alectoris rufa*)
8 Sardinian warbler
   (*Sylvia melanocephala*)
9 stonechat (*Saxicola torquata*)
10 woodchat shrike
   (*Lanius senator*)
11 woodlark (*Lullula arborea*)
12 tree pipit (*Anthus trivialis*)

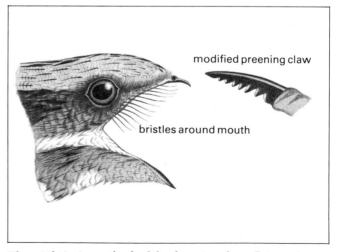

The nightjar's method of feeding involves flying about with its huge mouth open catching insects. The bristles assist food capture. A special claw helps to groom the bird and remove moth scales.

largely nocturnal, and they fly about after moths trying to catch them in their huge gaping mouths, which they use like an aerial butterfly net. Beautifully camouflaged by day, were it not for their distinctive prolonged churring evening song, most nightjars could well go undetected.

The thorny bushes – gorse and also hawthorn – provide safe nest sites but give another heathland bird, the red-backed shrike, a place to store food. In Britain, where sadly it is declining, the red-backed shrike is also called 'butcher bird', from its habit of impaling prey (insects largely, but also small mammals and birds) on thorns for later consumption. In some heathland areas, two other declining species of north-west Europe may also occur: the strange wryneck (a relative of the woodpeckers) which is as well camouflaged as the nightjar and feeds on ants; and the stone curlew, a strange-looking and stealthily moving wader that usually nests far from water.

The predator typical of heathland is undoubtedly the hobby, a small falcon with long, sickle-shaped wings. Although fast enough to catch a swift on the

Shrikes are often named butcher birds, due to their habit of impaling prey on thorns. These stores of food are called larders. Here a woodchat shrike impales a bumble bee for later consumption.

wing, many hobbies feed frequently on large insects such as dragonflies. Whilst the open heath provides good feeding for this migrant falcon, it needs the pine trees in which to build its nest.

## MAQUIS AND ITS BIRDS

The Mediterranean basin has a unique type of thorny scrub, perhaps better known under its French name *maquis* – from whence came the name of the wartime French resistance movement, whose members sought shelter in its impenetrable tangles. An interesting group of one of the warbler families also specializes in living in this habitat, and some are among the most ubiquitous and characteristic of Mediterranean birds. All lurk deep in the cover, but are inquisitive, emerging briefly into sight to inspect any intruders in their domain. In spring, they tend to be more visible as they emerge to sing, either perched or in a jerky, parachuting song-flight. All belong to the genus *Sylvia*, whose members include the more familiar whitethroat and blackcap, which are also Mediterranean residents. Most widespread of the exclusively Mediterranean species are the large orphean warbler – a greyish bird with a staring white eye and a melodious, thrush-like song – the boldly black-capped Sardinian warbler and the subdued but attractive mouse-like subalpine warbler. Dartford warblers (of which there is a tiny, outlying resident population on some remaining southern British heaths) occur in the west of the region.

The scrubland also covers the rocky outcrops that extend into the arid hill regions. Here, those familiar with common wheatears only, will be impressed by the addition of black-eared wheatears. Black redstarts can be seen in typical scree habitat (even though they are so much a feature of Mediterranean town rooftops) as can the inconspicuous rock sparrow, better identified by its white tail spots than its yellow throat patch. Also present are elegant rock buntings, moving tantalizingly in and out of sight among the rocks. High up, too, may be crag martins and alpine swifts, but these may also be seen (like the black redstart) using towns as an acceptable substitute habitat!

Bursts of tuneful, clear, fluting song can usually be traced to one of the rock thrushes, perched high on a crag or rock buttress. The blue rock thrush, slate blue all over, resides year-round in the Mediterranean basin and tends to occur at lower altitudes – in arid regions and near the coast. The slightly smaller migrant rock thrush, easily distinguished by its orange-chestnut tail and breast, is more of a mountain bird, breeding usually above 3000 ft (900 m) in altitude and ranging considerably further to the north than its cousin.

imm.

◄ **HOBBY** *Falco subbuteo*
**Length** 11 in (28 cm).
**Appearance** Adults dark slate-grey above, conspicuously white on side of neck; black moustachial streak; underparts pale, heavily dark-streaked; thighs chestnut. Young birds browner, lacking chestnut thighs.
**Distribution** Widespread summer visitor to Britain and Europe.

Hobbys are summer visitors, mainly confined to sandy heathland habitats, but also to farmland. Their long, sickle-shaped wings indicate a fast flight, and besides feeding on insects, hobbys often hunt around sand martin colonies. Such is their speed over short-distance pursuit dashes that they can even overhaul and kill swifts. Often they will take over an old crow's nest, particularly in a conifer, to lay their red-speckled eggs and raise a brood of about three young before a relatively early return migration to Africa.

**RED-LEGGED PARTRIDGE ►**
*Alectoris rufa*
**Length** 14 in (35 cm).

imm.

**Appearance** Adults sandy-brown, with bright pink beak and legs; throat and sides of face white, with broad black border; bold crescent-shaped white, black and brown marks on flanks. Young birds are much drabber.
**Distribution** Resident in west and south-west Europe, and Britain.

Red-legged partridges are native to the Iberian Peninsula. Their range has expanded northwards as far as southern England, but in large part as a result of artificial introductions. There have been many releases, and birds are artificially reared for sporting purposes. Some of those now being released are of similar, and related, Mediterranean and Asian species like the chukar (*A. chukar*), and hybrids do occur. All have calls based on the harsh 'chuck-aa' call that gives the chukar its name. They are birds of open grassy or ploughed fields, and chalky or sandy heathland. They lay ten to sixteen yellowish eggs spotted with brown in a shallow, well-concealed scrape.

**QUAIL** *Coturnix coturnix* ▲

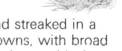

**Length** 7 in (18 cm).

**Appearance** Adults flecked and streaked in a mixture of sandy beiges and browns, with broad buff stripes on the crown. Males have a black bib. Young birds resemble females.

**Distribution** Widespread summer visitor to Britain and Europe.

Quail are summer migrants occurring in varying numbers from year to year but rarely common. The British Isles are at the climatic extreme of their European range and they are most often found on wide expanses of grassland or cereals on chalky soils. They are very secretive, far more often heard – with their distinctive 'whet-my-lips' call – than seen. Even the call is confusing when trying to pinpoint quail for they seem able to 'throw' their voices like ventriloquists. They lay seven to twelve whitish eggs, heavily blotched with brown.

## STONE CURLEW ▶
*Burhinus oedicnemus*
**Length** 16 in (40 cm).
**Appearance** Upperparts buff, streaked dark brown; wings dark with white bar; underparts buff, shading to white on belly; beak short, yellow and black; eye golden; legs yellow.
**Distribution** Breeds in Britain, northern and central Europe; winters in the south-west.

Stone curlews are now scarce breeding birds over much of Europe, restricted to wide-open dry areas such as chalk downs, sandy heaths, breckland and arid farmland. Both the birds and their eggs – usually three stone-coloured with dark marks – are extremely well camouflaged, and the birds move little during the day. Their large eyes give a clue to their nocturnal feeding activities, and their strange shrieking curlew-like calls are a feature of the night over huge cereal fields. In winter, they migrate south to Africa.

## BEE-EATER *Merops apiaster* ▶
**Length** 11 in (28 cm).
**Appearance** Unmistakeable; no other European bird has so many bright colours: chestnuts, blues, golds, greens, yellows and black; greenish tail with elongated central tail feathers, otherwise basically bluish below, gold above, with russet and blue wings.
**Distribution** Summer visitor to southern Europe.

As their name implies, bee-eaters hunt insects, including wasps and bees, which they stun and 'de-sting' by beating them on a branch. They are birds of warm, open sandy areas around the Mediterranean, migrating south to Africa for the winter. Sadly they are only occasional visitors to Britain and Ireland, although on a couple of occasions this century a handful of pairs have stayed to breed. Up to seven round, glossy white eggs are laid.

## ROLLER *Coracias garrulus* ▶
**Length** 12 in (30 cm).
**Appearance** Blue head and underparts; dark blue tail; back chestnut; wings black and electric blue, very obvious in flight. Young birds paler and drabber.
**Distribution** Summer visitor to southern and eastern Europe.

Rollers choose perches on bushes and trees in open dry country from which they drop down on to prey – spiders, beetles, grasshoppers and even lizards – passing beneath. They get their name from a tumbling aerobatic display flight, which shows the kingfisher-blue wings to best advantage. They are only scarce vagrants to Britain and Ireland. Rollers lay up to six round, white eggs in a single clutch.

◄ **NIGHTJAR** *Caprimulgus europaeus*
**Length** 11 in (28 cm).
**Appearance** Distinctly mottled with rich browns, greys, buffs and chestnuts above and below. Males have white patches on wings and tail.
**Distribution** Widespread summer visitor to many parts of Britain and Europe.

Nightjars are a diminishing species in many places; perhaps victims of the reclamation of marginal land, and perhaps declining because of subtle climatic changes. They have an unmistakeable continuous churring song and a display flight that includes noisy wing-claps. Nightjars are ground-nesters, laying up to three eggs, and are beautifully camouflaged against the heath or woodland litter. They rest during the day and hunt in the fading light of evening and the night, feeding on insects which they catch in their huge mouths, which open literally from ear to ear.

**CALANDRA LARK** *Melanocorypha calandra* ►
**Length** 8 in (20 cm).
**Appearance** Upperparts sandy brown with grey-buff and dark brown marks, underparts whitish with large dark marks on either side of the neck; in flight, wings and tail appear almost black with white margins.
**Distribution** Resident in the extreme south of Europe.

Calandra larks are among the largest of all larks, and are quite common in open, dry country in the extreme south of Europe, throughout the year. They are extremely rare vagrants to Britain and Ireland. The nest contains up to five greenish eggs, boldly spotted with brown.

◄ **SHORT-TOED LARK** _Calandrella cinerea_
**Length** 5 in (13 cm).
**Appearance** Upperparts mottled brown and pale sandy buff, underparts white, unstreaked except for dark smudges on sides of lower neck; dark centre to tail is conspicuous in flight.
**Distribution** Summer visitor to extreme south of Europe.

Short-toed larks are birds of arid grassland and dried-out mudflats and salt pans in the Mediterranean basin, migrating south into Africa for the winter. Their visits to Britain and Ireland are infrequent and spasmodic, and most are seen at bird observatories or in coastal areas. The nest usually contains three or four off-white eggs, profusely mottled with grey and brown.

**WOODLARK** _Lullula arborea_ ►
**Length** 6 in (15 cm).
**Appearance** Dark buff with brown streaks above; crown dark with fine black streaks, bold buff eye-stripes almost meeting on nape; buff, shading to white below, with dark streaks on breast.
**Distribution** Resident in south-western Europe; summer visitor elsewhere (including small numbers in Britain).

Although common residents of parts of the Continent of Europe, towards the north of their range sadly woodlarks are in a decline, particularly rapid in Britain. In part this is due to the destruction of their heathland habitat, primarily by encroaching farmland and the 'recovery' of so-called marginal land, but other factors, such as climatic change, are probably also important. The decrease of these summer migrants is particularly tragic, as they have a most beautiful fluting song, produced in song flight and containing long 'lu-lu-lu-lu-lu' phrases, from which their generic name _Lullula_ comes. Woodlarks usually lay three or four off-white eggs with red freckles.

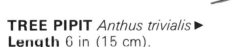

**TREE PIPIT** _Anthus trivialis_ ►
**Length** 6 in (15 cm).
**Appearance** Slightly larger, stockier and more upright than the meadow pipit, with a more yellow-buff breast; flesh-coloured legs; relatively short hind claw; call note and song are the best distinguishing features.
**Distribution** Widespread British and European summer visitor.

From mid-April to the end of July, male tree pipits defend their woodland territories with a distinctive song flight, fluttering skywards from a high songpost and then gliding down to the same or nearby perch. The shrill, musical, canary-like notes carry great distances. Trees, tall bushes or occasionally pylons are therefore essential habitat requirements, as well as open or rough areas in which they can find their insect prey. Despite the presence of suitable habitats, tree pipits have never bred in Ireland, although they are common in many parts of Scotland and Wales, and have recently spread to the Isle of Man. The call, a shrill, hoarse 'teeze', is the only certain method of identifying isolated individuals on migration between their African wintering grounds and summer breeding areas in Europe. Four to six speckled, brown, grey or reddish eggs are laid.

imm.  ♂

## WOODCHAT SHRIKE *Lanius senator* ▶
**Length** 7 in (18 cm).
**Appearance** Adult males distinctive, with chestnut crown and nape, black-and-white wings and tail and white rump and underparts. Females duller and less contrasting; buffish below. Juveniles resemble juvenile red-backed shrike but are paler with whitish, scaly shoulder patches.
**Distribution** Summer visitor to southern Europe.

These small, handsome shrikes breed around the Mediterranean, as well as east almost to India and north almost to the English Channel. They winter in tropical West Africa. In Britain and Ireland they are principally rare passage migrants: peak numbers occur in spring (May and June) and autumn (August and September), with relatively few being seen in April, July and October. Identification of adults is easy, but juveniles are well camouflaged without any bold markings and closely resemble young red-backed shrikes (*L. collurio*). Widespread in their choice of breeding habitat, woodchat shrikes can be found on open ground with scattered trees, scrubland, olive groves and even thick woodland. Like other shrikes, their calls are harsh and chattering, but the song is more melodious and often mimics other species. Six eggs, very variable in colour, are laid in one, occasionally two, broods.

**SARDINIAN WARBLER** _Sylvia melanocephala_ ▶
**Length** 6 in (15 cm).
**Appearance** Adult males upperparts grey
brown, with black hood and striking red eye-ring;
underparts white, shading to buff on flanks.
Females and young browner above, with less
distinct eye-ring.
**Distribution** Resident in south and south-west
Europe.

One of the commonest and most typical of the
warblers of Mediterranean hillside scrub. Although
often churring in alarm from deep inside the bushes,
Sardinian warblers are always active, and soon
emerge to look at an intruder. The male is
particularly conspicuous in spring, singing either in
flight or from the top of a bush, when his black-and-
white plumage is very striking. These sedentary
birds are rarely seen in the north and are extremely
scarce vagrants to Britain and Ireland. The nest
contains up to five greenish eggs, variably spotted
with grey or brown.

◀ **BARRED WARBLER** _Sylvia nisoria_
**Length** 6 in (15 cm).
**Appearance** Upperparts grey; head dark grey
with dark cheek and white eye; dark tail with
white outer feathers. Underparts barred, often
faintly. Young birds paler grey, barring on
underparts often faint and confined to flanks.
**Distribution** Summer visitor to east and north-
east Europe.

Barred warblers breed in open country such as
scrub or well-hedged farmland, and one of their
more curious features is their reputation for often
nesting fairly close to a pair of red-backed shrikes.
Outside their predominantly eastern breeding range
barred warblers are uncommon but often annual
visitors on migration, most being seen at coastal
bird observatories. Up to six pale greenish eggs,
finely freckled with lavender, are laid.

◄ **SUBALPINE WARBLER** *Sylvia cantillans*
**Length** 5 in (13 cm).
**Appearance** Adult males dark grey above, with brown wings and white-edged tail, which is frequently flicked; underparts russet, paler on belly; white moustachial streak; red eye-ring. Females and young similar but paler.
**Distribution** Summer visitor to south and south-west Europe.

A typically Mediterranean species, subalpine warblers are summer migrants to be found in scrub in low-lying areas and in woodland glades. It is difficult to obtain good views of these skulking birds except when the male indulges in his song flights, soaring high over the scrub and producing a whitethroat-like, but much more melodious, warble. Rarely venturing far north of the Mediterranean, subalpine warblers are very rare vagrants to Britain and Ireland. Up to five pale buff eggs with reddish spots are laid.

**DARTFORD WARBLER** *Sylvia undata* ►
**Length** 5 in (13 cm).
**Appearance** Upperparts dark grey, with long dark tail; underparts russet, with some white flecks on throat, paling to white on belly. Females rather duller. Young much browner.
**Distribution** Resident in the extreme west and south-west of Europe, and southern Britain.

Nowadays, Dartford warblers are never seen anywhere near Dartford Heath, where the first British specimens were shot. Typically they are birds of Mediterranean scrub and rough farmland, but populations extend northwards to Brittany. A small population is still resident in Britain, retaining the association with heathland and nesting in the few suitable sandy heaths in the south, where they lay five finely spotted whitish eggs. Unusually for warblers, they do not migrate and cannot escape the northern winter. Sudden heavy snowfalls, covering their food supply, can be devastating to the population.

**WHEATEAR** *Oenanthe oenanthe* ▶
**Length** 6 in (15 cm).
**Appearance** Adult males grey above, with dark eye-patch, black wings and black-and-white tail and rump; underparts pale cinnamon. Females browner. Young very scaly in appearance.
**Distribution** Summer visitor throughout Britain and Europe.

The name of the wheatear has nothing to do either with the cereal or the ear: it derives from two Saxon words, *whit* for white and *earse* for rump. Wheatears prefer open, short grass habitats, usually with little in the way of shrub cover, and often nest in a short underground tunnel. Normally five or six bluish eggs are laid, occasionally spotted with brown. Wheatears are double brooded in the south of their range. In an area without any songposts, they either use a prominent boulder or else produce their short scratchy warble during a brief up-and-down song flight.

**BLACK-EARED WHEATEAR** ▶
*Oenanthe hispanica*
**Length** 6 in (15 cm).
**Appearance** Adult males cinnamon brown above and below, with dark eye-patch (sometimes the whole face and throat are black), black wings and black-and-white tail and rump. Females browner. Young browner and more scaly.
**Distribution** Summer visitor to south and south-west Europe.

The commonest of the wheatear family in the Mediterranean basin, black-eared wheatears (which occur in two plumage variations – black-'eared' and black-throated) are birds of open rocky and sandy habitats. They are migrants to Europe from Africa, and the very occasional vagrants that reach Britain and Ireland are usually wind-driven overshooting migrants. Black-eared wheatears lay up to six blue-grey eggs with fine, red-brown spots.

**STONECHAT** *Saxicola torquata* ▲
**Length** 5 in (13 cm).
**Appearance** Adult males with black head, back
and tail; white rump and white bar on dark
wings; white collar and belly, breast orange.
Females and young browner and more streaked.

**Distribution** Resident in Britain and western
and southern Europe. Summer visitor to eastern
Europe.

Stonechats quickly draw attention to themselves by
chosing a prominent perch such as a bush-top, fence
or telephone wire, and 'chacking' loudly when an
intruder (of any shape or size) passes. This 'chack',
which sounds like two pebbles being struck
together, is the origin of their name, and is
accompanied by continuous flicking of both wings
and tail. Stonechats can be found in scrubby or
heathland areas, often near the coast. Up to six pale
blue, red-speckled eggs are laid, and there are at
least two broods.

## WHINCHAT _Saxicola rubetra_ ▶
**Length** 5 in (13 cm).
**Appearance** Adult males speckled brown and fawn above, with a white eye-stripe above dark cheek patch; wings and tail brown with white markings; breast pale orange. Females and young paler, less distinctly marked, more speckled.
**Distribution** Summer visitor to most parts of Britain and Europe.

Whinchats are widespread but never common breeding birds on rough grassland, downs and moorland fringes, and even bush-clad railway embankments. Their essential habitat requirements appear to be rough grassland with suitable post-and-wire fences or small hawthorn or gorse bushes. From these whinchats may sing their high-pitched warble (with snatches mimicked from other birds) and scan the ground beneath for passing prey – normally beetles, ants and similar invertebrates. A clutch of five or six deep blue eggs is laid, occasionally with fine freckles. Sometimes there are two broods.

## YELLOWHAMMER _Emberiza citrinella_ ▶
**Length** 7 in (18 cm).
**Appearance** Adult males upperparts chestnut, including rump; crown yellow; underparts golden-yellow with faint chestnut band across breast; head yellow with complex black line pattern on sides. Females and young streaked brown above, paler below; rump chestnut.
**Distribution** Resident in most parts of Britain and Europe.

Yellowhammers can be found on heaths, scrubby areas and extensive farmland hedgerows throughout Europe, where they are strikingly evident in high summer. At this time, the male is conspicuous both because of his plumage and because he produces his wheezy but characteristic 'little-bit-of-bread-and-no-cheese' song, the last syllable of which is long and drawn-out. In winter, when plumages are much drabber, yellowhammers are less obvious as they join other buntings and finches, often in large flocks, foraging on the ground for corn among the stubble or seeking out weed seeds on rough ground. Usually three to five eggs are laid; these have a variable, but pale ground colour with dark marks and spots.

# Woodlands

Deciduous woodland offers rich and varied niches for a great number of bird species – more, paradoxically, than when most of Europe was covered in dense, impenetrable tracts of forest. Coniferous woodland, although able to support less species, is nevertheless an important habitat for birds, especially the non-plantation variety.

Nowhere is the evidence of man's impact more dramatically apparent than in woodland. As recently as a thousand years ago much of the landscape was covered in extensive tracts of native hardwood trees, with native conifers like the pine widespread on sandy or upland soils. Today, in many European countries, this forest cover (variously estimated then at 60–80 per cent of the land surface) has been reduced to a mere 10 per cent or less, despite recent deliberate emphasis on re-afforestation schemes. In addition, particularly in the case of conifers, much of the new planting is of alien species introduced for their plantation timber qualities, and often these species are sited in areas that would naturally have supported deciduous trees.

## DECIDUOUS WOODLAND AND ITS BIRDS

The physical structure of a deciduous woodland plays a significant part in determining the species of birds which will be present. Today, this physical structure is often a direct result of management policy, but there are still many areas of semi-natural woodland where nature plays the major role in determining where there are clearings – caused when an aged tree has fallen – or where there is dense undergrowth. Basically, the greater the canopy (tree top) area, the more glades there are between the trees. This means that there will be a surface area for food and nest sites, and thus more birds (of more species) are likely to be encountered. Woodland margins are usually much richer in birds than the dark interior – but this dark interior should

1 long-eared owl (*Asio otus*)
2 sparrowhawk
   (*Accipiter nisus*)
3 crossbill (*Loxia curvirostra*)
4 great spotted woodpecker
   (*Dendrocopos major*)
5 jay (*Garrulus glandarius*)
6 nuthatch (*Sitta europaea*)
7 treecreeper (*Certhia familiaris*)

8 blackcap (*Sylvia atricapilla*)
9 goldcrest (*Regulus regulus*)
10 woodcock (*Scolopax rusticola*)
11 blue tit (*Parus caeruleus*)

not be excluded, as it also offers much of interest.

There are surprisingly few real woodland specialist birds, although some species may seem (for at least part of the year) to be very closely associated with a particular species of tree. An excellent example of this is the jay. Jays are members of the crow family, most of which are tree-nesters, but it is the jay which is perhaps the most typical and constant inhabitant of deciduous woodland, its harsh calls and bold white rump both well suited for contact and communication in the conditions of poor visibility that prevail in the undergrowth and in the tree canopy. Being omnivores, jays will take whatever food is available, in summer mixing worms and other soil animals from the leaf litter of the woodland floor with the eggs, nestlings and fledglings of other woodland birds. In autumn and winter the diet becomes more specific, as tree fruits (especially large, tough seeds like acorns) feature prominently. Ecologically, jays are often regarded as a major factor in the perpetuation and spread of oak woodland, because of their habit of picking acorns from the canopy and flying off some distance to bury them in soil as a food cache against extremes of winter climate. Many of the hidden acorns are not retrieved by the jays, and some subsequently germinate to produce new oaks.

The type of woodland affects considerably the bird species associated with it, and the widest variety of woodland birds are associated with broad-leaved, or deciduous, woodland consisting mainly of trees such as oak, elm, ash, beech, birch and sycamore. These woodlands usually support a varied undergrowth consisting of species such as bramble, hawthorn and elder, mixed with plenty of herbaceous plants. This provides good feeding and nesting areas for the population of small birds. It stands to reason that the amount of insect and plant food available is greater in this sort of wood than it would be in an area with little or no undergrowth, and this is the main reason that deciduous woodland often holds more birds than mature stands of conifer.

It would seem that deciduous woodland should offer excellent feeding to the seed-eating finches, but the wood itself is not particularly rich in small seeds, except where penetrated by clearances in which a grassy or herbaceous undergrowth can develop. This helps to explain the relatively small number of this large group of birds found deep in woodland proper. Although, as their colloquial name suggests, they rely heavily on seeds of various sizes to provide the bulk of their diet, most seed-eaters will take occasional flowers and fruitlets, and certainly unripe seeds from early-flowering plants such as dandelion, which become available when last season's seed stocks are at their lowest ebb.

In the breeding season, most finches feed their young (at least in the early stages of growth) on a protein-rich collection of various small insects. Perhaps to take best advantage of the high insect populations on the flush of leaf growth, most seed-eaters are mid-summer breeders. This allows them to build nests when trees are in leaf, providing maximum shelter.

The finches found in broad-leaved woods show as clear an ecological gradation of beak size and shape in relation to feeding as any other group in the world of birds. This gradation, coupled with a range of feeding sites extending from the woodland floor to the canopy, offers the main clues as to how these seed-eaters partition their food resources. All have basically triangular beaks and rounded skulls, with relatively strong muscles powering the jaw action for seed crushing. Smallest of the group, and with the smallest beak, is the redpoll. Redpolls feed mostly on the ground and on the seeds of small herbaceous plants and grasses. The chaffinch has a slightly larger and more pointed beak, and again feeds predominantly on the ground but on larger seeds. Next in the size scale comes the greenfinch, with an altogether stouter beak, wider and deeper in relation to its length, for crushing larger seeds on the plant or on the ground.

At the top of the scale are the heavy-headed, massive-beaked hawfinches, capable of crushing the stones of tree fruits like wild cherry and damson to extract the nutritious kernel within. Some are said to exert incredible pressures in excess of 200 lb per sq in (14 kg per cm$^2$)! The inside of the beak has strongly ridged grooves to hold the stones in a vice-like grip. Hawfinches spend much of their time in the canopy, descending to feed on fallen stones late in the winter. Rather more specialized is the goldfinch, which has tweezer-like, elongated mandibles for extracting seeds from the spine-protected seed heads of thistles and teazel. Another specialist is the bullfinch, with a beak more rounded in profile than the others. The peg-like tongue resembles that of the parrots, and beak and tongue combine to rotate flower buds, removing the outer scales so that the nutritious flower initial within can be eaten. Buds are a major food source for the bullfinch during the late winter, helping to avoid excessive feeding demands on a steadily diminishing seed crop under pressure from the other seed-eaters.

Old deciduous woodland takes on an additional character once its branches start to break off, its timber starts to soften and rot, and trees start to fall, for this all provides new niches for additional species to exploit. Elderly timber in woodland that is not managed with the 'hygiene' unfortunately so popular with commercial foresters shelters much more insect life, and falling trees leave gaps in the

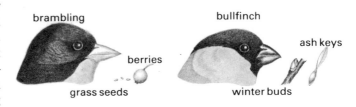

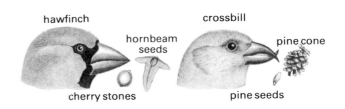

Four species of finch with bill modifications reflecting their different diets.

canopy so that patches of undergrowth can further develop. Holes can be made in such trees by woodpeckers, anxious to nest or to remove the grubs of boring insects. These nest holes, used perhaps once or twice by woodpeckers, are then used by a variety of other species. The green woodpecker is as much a bird of park or farmland as of woods, since its main food is ants. With the loss of so much permanent grassland there are generally fewer ants to be found, and green woodpeckers are only very slowly recovering from the effects of recent cold winters. The two spotted woodpeckers – greater and lesser – have suffered less severely. Great spotted woodpeckers are quite common in many areas, and regularly visit country garden bird-tables. Lesser spotted woodpeckers are much less conspicuous birds, as well as being considerably smaller (chaffinch-size), and are often considered to be rare.

Species exploiting old woodpecker holes include jackdaws, starlings, and many tit species – the commonest users being great tits and blue tits. Only one tit – the willow tit – regularly digs its own nest hole, and this is usually in soft rotten timber. Its near relative, the marsh tit, uses old woodpecker holes and natural crevices. The two species are generally regarded as difficult to separate: very similar in plumage, the willow tit has a rather thicker-set neck and a pale buffish patch on the otherwise brown feathers of the closed wing, but the best way to distinguish them is by the call – the marsh tit's is a strident 'pitch-you', and the willow tit's a rather diffident 'dee, dee, dee'.

Another deciduous woodland 'specialist' is perhaps the least expected. The woodcock is so unlike the rest of the wader family in habits and habitat that it holds a special fascination for birdwatchers. For a start, its preferred habitat is woodland, winter and summer alike, and not the marshes of the mudflats. Most favoured are woods with a deep layer of leaf litter, with some areas of dry ground suitable for nesting and some expanses of damp soil for feeding. These wet areas, rich in the worms which are the major item in the woodcock's diet, are usually kept perpetually moist by seepage from underground springs. Beside this mixture of wet and dry ground, woodcocks also require open glades for their display flights.

Although, because of its excellent camouflage, the woodcock may be difficult to spot, once seen it is very distinctive, with a delicately streaked and mottled rich brown plumage, absolutely ideal for camouflage against a background of dead leaves or bracken. Usually, whether on the nest or feeding, the woodcock will rely on this amazing camouflage and crouch down, unmoving, until approached so close that it is about to be stood on. It has a disproportionately large beak – about 3 in (7.5 cm) long – and probes in the soft soil for earthworms and insect larvae such as leatherjackets. The rather swollen tip of the beak contains numerous sensitive nerve endings which allow the woodcock to identify its prey and there is a special skull adaptation which enables it to avoid taking a mouthful of mud or soil with each worm. The nasal bones (which support the upper part of the beak) are long and flexible, and not rigidly attached to the roof of the skull between the eyes. Special muscles can pull the nasal bones back, allowing just the tip of the beak to open and the worm to be grasped and eaten.

## CONIFEROUS WOODLAND AND ITS BIRDS

Apart from the primeval and vast tracts of forest in the far north, most coniferous woodland today is very varied, and its bird populations likewise. Some areas of primeval coniferous forest also remain further south, however, notably the Caledonian pinewoods of the Highlands of Scotland. Within this 'living antique' of a forest, under serious threat of extinction by the pressures to introduce commercially viable conifer plantations to replace it, widely distributed woodland birds such as chaffinches flourish, as do conifer-dwelling species such as coal tits. Two species in particular also make this forest their home – the crested tit and the Scottish pine crossbill. Of all the tits, crested tits seem the best adapted to life in coniferous woods, and are even capable of excavating their own nest hole. In Continental Europe they are very widely distributed in a variety of conifer types stretching from the Mediterranean coasts north to Scandinavia. Crested tits are, however, extremely sedentary, and it may be that their limited range in Scotland is a reflection of the reduced state of their ancestral home forests, to which they have become closely adapted over the ages, and that their lack of mobility prevents the colonization of the 'new' conifer forests in England by immigrants from over the Channel.

The crossbill family (which pose as many problems for taxonomists as they do to birdwatchers) are a fascinating group found throughout the available coniferous woodland. The Scottish pine crossbill is another example of close adaptation to a particular tree species. In the northern hemisphere the woody cones of the various native conifers – larch, spruce and pine – are exploited by this very specialized family of birds capable of extracting the seeds from between the rigid wooden 'flakes' of the cones. In Scandinavia and to the east, it is the two-barred crossbill that specializes in the small, relatively flexible cones of the larch, and the common crossbill that tackles the cones of spruce, which are rather larger and tougher. In keeping with the tasks they have to perform, the beaks of these two birds differ in size and thus strength, though retaining the same flattened, cross-tipped profile that allows them to snip out the seeds from the cones with ease, and which gives the family its name. Largest of all is the parrot crossbill, capable of dealing with the massive cones of European pines; but only slightly smaller is the Scottish pine crossbill, adapted by long isolation to feeding from the cones of the Scots pine. Interestingly, Scottish pine crossbills, like crested tits, are sedentary and are rarely, if ever, seen outside the Caledonian forest.

The common crossbill has evolved a migration stratagem that assists its survival when food becomes scarce. This normally occurs after a series of good breeding seasons on the Continent, when numbers are high and pressures increase on the remaining stocks of cones. After the breeding season, many birds move away west, sometimes travelling only a short distance before adequate food is found, but at other times moving in numbers across the Channel and settling in the 'new' forests of south and east England.

Because they feed in the tops of tall, mature, cone-bearing conifers which are evergreen and carry long needle-shaped leaves, and because many of the birds are females or young and thus yellowish or greenish brown in colour, obtaining a good view of feeding crossbills is not always easy. They have a parrot-like, heavy-headed appearance and also a parrot-like agility as they reach towards a new cone,

The turkey-sized capercaillie has an extraordinary, clumsy display dance accompanied by a song which sounds like a cork being drawn from a bottle.

often hanging upside down. They are relatively quiet when feeding, although using an explosive 'chip' flight call, but one giveaway that crossbills are about overhead is the occasional dropping of partially eaten, slightly shredded cones to the forest floor. Interestingly, their nesting season is geared more to the availability of good supplies of suitable food than to our concept of 'the seasons'. In consequence crossbills may often breed very early, sometimes sitting on eggs in late November or December, with snow lying on the back of the incubating female!

Until a few years ago it was fashionable to condemn mature plantations of alien conifer species as being virtually devoid of bird life. The trees were planted so close that even the rides between plantation blocks seemed like grey canyons, muffling all sounds save the sighing of the wind. It seemed that woodpigeons, coal tits and chaffinches were the major avian inhabitants, and these only in low numbers. As more and more of these plantations are explored (and the paths in many are open freely to the public) attitudes are changing, and there is now plenty of evidence that, even when mature, conifer plantations may be a perfectly suitable habitat, supporting quite a reasonable number of diverse species including thrushes, warblers, tits, birds of prey and owls. There are also particular attractions such as the crossbill, which has been joined in recent years by the firecrest as a bird worthy of special birdwatching attention.

The first ten to fifteen years in the life of a newly planted conifer plantation produces a particularly rich habitat: the trees are not tall enough to shade out smaller plants, food abounds, and shelter is plentiful as the trees are planted so close together. Thus the despair with which many country-lovers, as well as birdwatchers, tend to greet the new plantation should always be tempered with an eager expectation of the benefits of the first few years, and

with the knowledge that the gloomy conditions will not last for ever, as commercial forestry blocks will be felled regularly for timber and subsequently replanted. At the moment one or two scarce species are benefiting greatly from such newly planted blocks: for instance sparrowhawks are increasing now in the west and north after the disastrous 1960s when the ravages of poisoning by agrochemicals were most felt.

There are some species, like tree pipits and nightjars, that should also be expected during the first couple of years after the new planting. Other scrubland species soon begin to appear, becoming more common as time goes by – linnets, goldfinches, bullfinches, blackbirds, wrens, dunnocks and whitethroats are a few examples. As the cover begins to develop, one or two more interesting, and perhaps slightly unexpected, species begin to appear: the skulking but very handsome lesser whitethroat, and the reed bunting and the grasshopper warbler – the latter birds more often associated with rather wetter areas. In the remoter areas of the west and north, you may be lucky enough to see a hunting hen harrier, regularly patrolling its beat on rather stiff wings or, at dusk, a long-eared owl looking for roosting birds or foraging for field mice or voles.

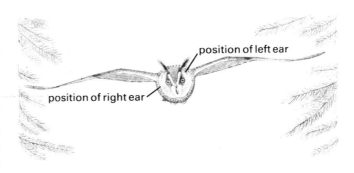

The conspicuous feather tufts of the long-eared owl have nothing to do with hearing. The true ears lie behind the facial disc, and are asymmetrically positioned for accurate sound location.

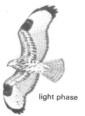

light phase

◀ **BUZZARD** *Buteo buteo*
**Length** 21 in (53 cm).
**Appearance** Usually dark brown above, paler below but heavily marked; underwing shows a dark patch at the carpal joint or 'wrist'; plumage is very variable, with some very dark and some very pale individuals.
**Distribution** Resident throughout most of Britain and Europe.

Buzzards are the commonest large soaring bird, and are resident year-round over mountain, moorland and farmland in western and northern Britain, although they are strangely very scarce in Ireland. Although they suffered a setback when the disease myxomatosis drastically reduced rabbit numbers – their main prey – buzzards are making a come-back and extending their range eastward. Broad, fingered wings and a short tail often held rounded, like a fan, help buzzards to circle slowly in the upcurrents. During the breeding season, loud, drawn-out mewing calls help identification. Usually lay two or three red-blotched white eggs in a single brood.

♂            ♀

◀ **SPARROWHAWK** *Accipiter nisus*
**Length** 12–15 in (30–38 cm).
**Appearance** Males dark grey above; white, closely barred with chestnut below. Females considerably larger: grey-brown above; white, barred with grey below, with clear white eye-stripe. Young birds browner, and more heavily marked below.
**Distribution** Resident throughout most of Britain and Europe.

Sparrowhawks are increasing again after a decline caused by agrochemical pollution. They are birds of woodland and scrub, catching other birds for food. They may perch in wait, or patrol quietly down the hedgerows, dashing in pursuit of suitable quarry, their short, rounded wings giving them the acceleration and manoeuvrability they need to catch it, no matter how much it twists and turns. They lay up to six white eggs, blotched and streaked with dark brown, in a single clutch.

**Distribution** Resident throughout most of Britain and Europe.

Commoner in the larger expanses of forest on the Continent than in Britain, the status of the goshawk is changing. Once it was a rare migrant, but there are now increasing numbers of breeding pairs, some of them wild, others probably originating as escapes from falconers' collections. Goshawks look and behave like massive, solidly built but short-tailed sparrowhawks (*A. nisus*), preferring coniferous woodland and selecting larger prey, females tackling birds up to the size of a capercaillie! They lay up to four off-white eggs in a single clutch.

**GOSHAWK** *Accipiter gentilis* ▲
**Length** 19–24 in (48–60 cm).
**Appearance** Males and females have similar plumage, but females appreciably larger in size; slate-grey above with a marked white eye-stripe, white with grey barring below; the white undertail coverts are a key feature.

### RED KITE *Milvus milvus* ▲
**Length** 24–26 in (60–65 cm).
**Appearance** Rufous above and below, paler on the head; deeply forked chestnut tail is diagnostic; wings long and slender with white patches on the undersides.
**Distribution** Summer visitor to central Europe; resident in some isolated areas of Europe north of the Mediterranean (including Wales).

Red kites breed in deciduous woodlands, often in remote, steep-sided valleys, ranging in search of carrion or hunting over the hills, moors and nearby farmland. Although in Britain the isolated resident population is still only a couple of dozen strong, red kites are enjoying a run of several years' successful production of young. However, rigorous protection is still needed to keep their future secure against the threats of traps, poison baits (usually set to kill crows) and egg collectors. Up to five white eggs, spotted with brown, are laid in one clutch.

### HONEY BUZZARD *Pernis apivorus* ▲
**Length** 21 in (53 cm).
**Appearance** Adults and young plumage very variable from dark brown to cream; mostly grey-headed; dark brown back, white-streaked brown below; tail long, straight-sided, with broad bars; underside of wings pale, with dark patch at 'wrist'.
**Distribution** Summer visitor to central and southern Europe (including Britain).

Summer visitors to Britain, honey buzzards have a British stronghold in the New Forest, Hampshire, where a few pairs breed, but otherwise nesting is occasional and by solitary pairs. Up to three white eggs, heavily speckled with red, are laid. As their name suggests, honey buzzards specialize in feeding on bee and wasp nests, consuming combs, honey and grubs. The grey head feathers are unusually hard and offer some protection against the stings as the honey buzzards dig out the nest.

### ◄ BLACK KITE *Milvus migrans*
**Length** 21 in (53 cm).
**Appearance** Adults and young varying shades of dark brown, pale patches on wings; long tail only shallowly forked.
**Distribution** Summer visitor to central and southern Europe.

Although only occasional visitors to Britain and Ireland, black kites are regular summer visitors over much of central and southern Europe, becoming more numerous, and remaining year-round, in warmer countries. Black kites are extremely agile in flight, with long legs able to snatch up a sunning fish from the surface of a lake, or, increasingly in urban surrounds, to snatch a sandwich from an unguarded plate during a picnic! Up to five white eggs, spotted red-brown, are laid in one clutch.

**WOODCOCK** _Scolopax rusticola_ ▶
**Length** 14 in (35 cm).
**Appearance** Adults and young richly mottled with fawns, browns and chestnut above; paler below, barred greyish-brown; head is angular in shape, with crosswise buff stripes.
**Distribution** Breeds in northern and central Europe (including Britain); winters in south and south-west.

Woodcocks are an exception among waders in that their prime habitat choice, throughout the year, is mature woodland, where they probe deeply in moist soil for the worms which form the bulk of their food. They are well camouflaged against the brown leaf-litter background when feeding or sitting on their nest. They usually lay four eggs, which are buff or brown with darker spots and squiggles. In spring, the birds patrol a regular 'beat' through the woodland glades in an evening display flight called roding. Their wings are rounded and the flight almost moth-like, and they produce frog-like croakings and bat-like 'tsee-wick' calls.

**CAPERCAILLIE** _Tetrao urogallus_ ▶
**Length** 34 in (85 cm); females 24 in (60 cm).
**Appearance** Males huge and unmistakeable, like an iridescent black turkey. Females lack the fan-shaped tail, and have buffish-brown mottled plumage. Young birds resemble females.
**Distribution** Resident in north, north-east and central Europe (including Britain).

One of the most striking residents of coniferous forests in Britain. By sheer weight alone male capercaillies can break down young trees and cause considerable damage as they clamber about in the treetops seeking tender young spruce shoots for food. In spring, the rattling song, terminating in a 'pop' like a cork drawn from a bottle, seems feeble for the size of the bird. The male, fluffed up to the full to be as intimidating as possible, has been known actually to prevent people entering his territory and may even try to keep out vehicles. Five to eight yellowish, sparsely brown-flecked eggs are laid.

## STOCK DOVE *Columba oenas* ▶
**Length** 13 in (33 cm).
**Appearance** Dull grey above and below; two dark bars on the wings; green and bronze iridescent feathers on neck and breast.
**Distribution** Resident in Britain, western and southern Europe; summer visitor only to north and north-east Europe.

Stock doves can be found on farmland, open woods and occasionally even on sea cliffs, and seem at the present time to be increasing, despite the advances of farming technology that threaten other species. They are hole-nesting birds – normally using natural cavities in trees or holes in old buildings – but in remote or treeless terrain they will occupy disused rabbit burrows. They lay up to three white eggs, and normally produce two or three broods. Outside the breeding season, many feed in small flocks on arable farmland, often in company with woodpigeons.

**Distribution** Resident in Britain, western and southern Europe; summer visitor to north and north-east Europe.

Woodpigeons are basically woodland birds, but have adapted to farmland hedgerows and will nest even in stunted bushes in remote and exposed coastal areas, the nest being a fragile 'see-through' flat platform of twigs in which two glossy white eggs are laid in two broods. In winter, woodpigeons tend to gather in flocks and if food is short, may feed upon crops, particularly brassicas, causing considerable damage. Others have completely spurned the rural life and have adapted well to urban areas, nesting in parks and feeding on scraps.

## WOODPIGEON *Columba palumbus* ▼
**Length** 16 in (40 cm).
**Appearance** Adults various shades of grey; bold white crescent-shaped wing-bar; white collar patch; pinkish tinge to breast and iridescent green-and-purple sheen on neck. Young birds lack white collar patches and iridescence.

**TURTLE DOVE** *Streptopelia turtur* ▶
**Length** 11 in (28 cm).
**Appearance** Crown grey; back mottled black-and-bronze; wings dark brown; tail black with narrow white tip; underparts pinkish grey, shading to white; black-and-white chequered collar marks.
**Distribution** Summer visitor to most parts of Britain and Europe, except the extreme north.

The Bible contains some of the earliest references to bird migration, for in the *Song of Solomon* the line '. . . turtle is heard in our land' refers not to the marine reptile but to the turtle dove. Turtle doves are small, fast-flying pigeons, widespread as a breeding summer visitor in southern and eastern England, but passage migrants elsewhere. Although they feed on farmland, turtle doves are open woodland birds, and the call is a peacefully drowsy purring, permeating the woodland glades. Up to three white eggs are laid, normally in two broods.

**CUCKOO** *Cuculus canorus* ▶
**Length** 13 in (33 cm).
**Appearance** Grey above (very rarely rufous); white below with grey barring; tail long and dark with white marks. Young birds darker, with white barring above.
**Distribution** Summer visitor to all parts of Britain and Europe; winters in Africa.

Cuckoos are fascinating birds with a parasitic life-cycle. When they return from their winter quarters in Africa, the female seeks out the nests of smaller birds which will act as foster parents to her offspring (commonly reed warblers in marshes, meadow pipits on moorland and dunnocks in farmland and woodland). She may lay up to 18 eggs in different nests. Even a cuckoo laying for the first time chooses the right host, matching the colour of her eggs with those already in the nest. The young cuckoo hatches quickly, and is soon strong enough to heave its foster brothers and sisters out of the nest. The young cuckoo grows quickly, receiving food from both of its foster parents, but does not migrate until some weeks after the adult cuckoos have departed. The fledgling cuckoo reaches Africa unaided, by pure instinctive navigation.

61

**PYGMY OWL** *Glaucidium passerinum* ▲
**Length** 7 in (18 cm).
**Appearance** Upperparts brown, spotted with white; underparts pale buff streaked with brown; facial disc has concentric dark rings; white 'eyebrow' marks; eyes yellow.
**Distribution**
Resident in north and north-east Europe.

These tiny owls are residents of dense coniferous woodlands, and often hunt during the day. For their size, they are voracious and aggressive hunters, tackling birds at least as big as themselves. They are sedentary birds, unlikely to be recorded in Britain and Ireland. The nest contains up to ten round, white eggs.

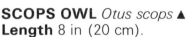

**SCOPS OWL** *Otus scops* ▲
**Length** 8 in (20 cm).
**Appearance** Uniformly brown, sometimes grey-tinged, sometimes chestnut; fine grey, black-and-white streaks; pale facial disc edged with black, slightly tufted or 'eared'; eyes yellow.
**Distribution** Breeds in extreme south of Europe.

Common in parks, gardens and woodlands in southern Europe, where their monotonous 'peeoo . . peeoo' whistling call is a feature of warm summer evenings. Scops owls are very scarce vagrants to Britain and Ireland. They have finely vermiculated plumage, which provides superb camouflage against a tree trunk. This is particularly effective if the bird is disturbed, when it makes itself slim and upright and becomes even harder to see. Scops owls are mostly insectivorous and nocturnal in habit. They lay usually four or up to six round white eggs.

ase                                    grey phase

**TAWNY OWL** *Strix aluco* ▶▲
**Length** 15 in (38 cm).
**Appearance** Brown or chestnut above, buff below, mottled and finely streaked with rich browns and buffs; facial disc pale, outlined in black; eyes dark.
**Distribution** Resident in most parts of Britain and Europe.

These are the commonest and most widespread owls in Britain and Europe (but strangely absent from Ireland). Tawny owls have adapted well to man-made changes in their ancestral deciduous woodland habitat. They can be found on farmland, and are inhabitants of many city centres, finding nest sites in old churches or hollow trees in parks and abundant food in the form of house sparrows and mice. Tawny owls start their display calling — the nocturnal spine-chilling 'to-whit, to-whoo-oo-oo' — soon after Christmas and breed early in the year. Usually up to five round, white eggs are laid in a single brood. The young remain dependent on their parents for about three months after fledging, during which time they are taught to hunt.

## LONG-EARED OWL *Asio otus* ▶
**Length** 14 in (35 cm).
**Appearance** Dark chestnut-brown, finely marked with buffs and browns; conspicuous feather tufts over eyes; facial disc brown, edged with black; eyes golden.
**Distribution** Widespread resident in most parts of Britain and Europe; summer visitor only in extreme north.

Long-eared owls are year-round woodland residents (preferring conifers) in Britain and Ireland, and numbers are augmented by winter visitors from the Continent, which may form roosts in woods or even scrub or orchards. Owls have extremely well-developed eyes, adapted for low-light vision, but they depend even more on their ears when hunting after dark. The ears of long-eared owls occupy much of the skull — the tufts on the head are not ears — and are asymmetrically placed to allow them to locate the tiniest scuffle of a mouse or vole. Experiments have demonstrated the pinpoint accuracy of their audio-location, even in absolute darkness. Normally up to six white eggs are laid in a single brood.

## HOOPOE ▶
*Upupa epops*
**Length** 11 in (28 cm).
**Appearance** Sandy-fawn above and on the breast, whitish on belly; long, black-tipped orange-fawn crest, often erected on landing; back, tail and rounded wings strikingly barred with black-and-white.
**Distribution** Summer visitor to most of Europe except the north.

Like several other colourful European birds, hoopoes are summer visitors to the Mediterranean area, penetrating well into France and, in the east, as far north as Latvia. Their slow, flopping flight, showing the strikingly barred wings, is characteristic, as is their habit of allowing close approach on the ground and feeding on prey as varied as ants and lizards. The nest, into which eight dirty white eggs are laid, is made in a tree hole and is usually extremely smelly. Hoopoes are annual visitors in small numbers to Britain and Ireland – especially the south coasts – in spring and autumn, and pairs occasionally remain to breed.

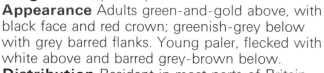

## ◀ GREEN WOODPECKER *Picus viridis*
**Length** 12 in (30 cm).
**Appearance** Adults green-and-gold above, with black face and red crown; greenish-grey below with grey barred flanks. Young paler, flecked with white above and barred grey-brown below.
**Distribution** Resident in most parts of Britain and Europe, except extreme north.

Green woodpeckers are widely distributed in open woodland and grassy farmland in England and Wales. They are scarce in lowland Scotland and absent from Ireland. In recent years these attractive birds, with their deeply undulating flight, have diminished in numbers, perhaps partly because they suffer severe mortality in cold winters. A more persistent cause of their decline is likely to be the general improvement (in agricultural terms) in grassland management. Old meadows, lumpy with ant hills, are now a scarcity and it is on ants that green woodpeckers often feed, pulling them out of their runs with a long tongue covered in sticky saliva. The tree hole nest contains up to seven round white eggs.

64

## GREAT SPOTTED WOODPECKER ▲
*Dendrocopos major*
**Length** 9 in (23 cm).
**Appearance** Adults black-and-white above,
male with a scarlet patch on the nape; underparts
white, scarlet beneath tail. Young birds are greyer,
with scarlet crown.
**Distribution** Resident in most parts of Britain
and Europe.

Like the other woodpeckers, great spotted woodpeckers are absent from Ireland. They have
powerful beaks, which they use like a hammer and
chisel to excavate a nest hole, often in living timber,
and to probe for the insect grubs upon which they
feed. Woodpeckers have very long tongues, which
when not in use are coiled in a special sheath on top
of the skull. The tongue is extended into the tunnels
bored by insects, and the prey is extracted with the
harpoon-like barbed tip. The tree-hole nest contains
up to seven white eggs.

## BLACK WOODPECKER *Dryocopus martius* ▶
**Length** 18 in (45 cm).
**Appearance** Plumage all black except for the
crimson crown, larger in males than females; beak
whitish, black-tipped.
**Distribution** Resident in north, east and central
Europe.

At least as large as a carrion crow – but with the
typical woodpecker undulating flight and head-up
perching habits as they search tree trunks for food –
black woodpeckers must be classified as 'unmistakeable'. They are widespread in old woodlands in
central and northern Europe, both coniferous and
broad-leaved. Despite a number of mistaken
sightings, a fully authenticated record has yet to
occur in Britain and Ireland.

### LESSER SPOTTED WOODPECKER▶
*Dendrocopos minor*
**Length** 6 in (15 cm).
**Appearance** Black with ladder-like white bars above, males with scarlet crown; white below, streaked brown on the flanks.
**Distribution** Resident in most parts of Britain and Europe, absent from Scotland.

These sparrow-sized woodpeckers prefer open deciduous woods, parks, orchards and farmland with plenty of trees. They have the typical woodpecker features of a specially strengthened tail (which serves as a prop when it moves, always head-up, on the tree) and strong claws arranged with two facing forward and two facing back for a better grip.

Both lesser and great spotted woodpeckers (*D. major*) 'drum' to indicate the borders of their territories, hammering on a resonant dead branch with their beaks. The lesser spotted woodpecker's rapid 'drum-roll' is higher pitched than that of the great spotted. The tree-hole nest contains four to six white eggs.

◀ **WRYNECK** *Jynx torquilla*
**Length** 7 in (18 cm).
**Appearance** Upperparts a finely vermiculated and streaked mixture of browns, fawns and black; underparts pale buff with darker crescent-shaped bars; tail brown, with several black-and-white bars.
**Distribution** Summer visitor to many parts of Britain and Europe.

Wrynecks are a summer visitor to most of Europe, including south-east England, and occasional passage migrants elsewhere. They feed on the ground, often on ants, and have a distinctive habit of turning their heads in slow motion at all sorts of angles as they feed, giving rise to the colloquial name 'snake bird'. For reasons not well understood, but perhaps associated with the loss of suitable feeding areas such as sandy heaths, the removal of old orchards with plenty of nest holes, and with subtle changes in climate, wrynecks have just become extinct as a breeding bird in England. Where breeding does occur, seven to ten round white eggs are laid.

## GOLDEN ORIOLE _Oriolus oriolus_ ▶
**Length** 10 in (25 cm).
**Appearance** Adult males unmistakeable; starling-like but with golden body and black-and-gold wings and tail. Females and young greenish-yellow above, white below with brownish streaks on breast.
**Distribution** Widespread summer visitor.

For all their apparently startlingly conspicuous plumage, male golden orioles are surprisingly well camouflaged as they flit about in the sunlit canopy of the trees in their deciduous woodland, parkland or olive grove habitat. Summer visitors to much of Europe, most golden orioles seen in the north and west are migrants blown off-course or overshooting their breeding grounds. Occasionally some pairs do remain to breed in these areas, such as southern Britain. Golden orioles are best detected by the male's loud fluty whistling 'weela-weeoo' call. Up to five white eggs with black spots are laid.

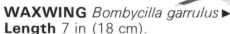

## WAXWING _Bombycilla garrulus_ ▶
**Length** 7 in (18 cm).
**Appearance** Sandy-brown, darker above than below, with black bib and eye-patch; rufous crest; yellow-tipped black tail and yellow-and-white pattern dark wings.
**Distribution** Breeds in extreme north and north-east, winters in north and central Europe (including Britain).

Close views of waxwings are needed to see the small red feather tips in the wings, looking like blobs of sealing wax, after which they are named. Waxwings breed in the forests of the extreme north of Europe, and visit western Europe during the winter. The numbers arriving are governed by food shortages on the Continent, and occasionally large numbers of waxwings (known as irruptions) may occur, often visiting gardens to feed on the fruits of shrubs such as cotoneaster and crab apples.

## NUTCRACKER _Nucifraga caryocatactes_ ▶
**Length** 13 in (33 cm).
**Appearance** Body grey-brown, boldly flecked with white; crown dark; rump and tail with conspicuous black-and-white pattern.
**Distribution** Sporadic winter visitor to north and north-east Europe.

Nutcrackers are birds of the conifer forests of northern and central Europe, usually finding sufficient food in the conifer cones and from the seeds and nuts of deciduous trees to survive the winter without undue difficulty. The nest contains three to five blue-green eggs, spotted with lavender. Only in occasional years of severe food shortage will they arrive in the west, ranging as far as Britain.

## JAY *Garrulus glandarius* ▶
**Length** 14 in (35 cm).
**Appearance** Upperparts rich pinkish buff; rump white; underparts paler, shading to white below all-black tail; crown with black streaks, black moustachial stripe; wings black, white and blue.
**Distribution** Resident throughout Britain and Europe.

Jays are among the most colourful of our birds, in marked contrast to most other members of the crow family. They are woodland and parkland birds, rarely seen far from mature trees with suitable seeds for their food, such as oak, beech, hornbeam and hazel. They are notorious nest-robbers during the summer, but turn to feeding on seeds in the autumn. They hide food in caches for the oncoming winter, and can often be seen flapping away, acorn in beak, intent on burying it for later use. It is often said that as they relocate so few acorns, this helps to spread oak woods, rather than assist jay survival. Normally five or six greenish eggs with dense dark mottling are laid, in a single clutch.

◀ **WREN** *Troglodytes troglodytes*
**Length** 4in (10 cm).
**Appearance** Males, females and juveniles have similar plumage: chestnut above, buff below, with fine black bars; beak slender, slightly down-curved; brown legs relatively robust and well adapted to their largely terrestrial life-style; wings rounded and short; flight swift, whirring and direct.
**Distribution** Widespread resident throughout Britain and Europe.

Wrens are adaptable birds, and bursts of their astonishingly ebullient song can be heard not only from typical farm, garden and woodland habitats, but also from reed-beds and coastal cliffs. Their small size, jauntily cocked tail and jerky, bustling movements as they seek insect prey in crevices among plants or rocks all help in identification. The male builds several well-concealed domed nests with a side entrance, the female choosing one and adding a lining of feathers. Two clutches are normal, each of four to six tiny white eggs, freckled with red. Although numbers soon recover, wrens suffer severe mortality in hard winters: at such times they may roost communally, and over 60 have been recorded in one nestbox.

## DUNNOCK *Prunella modularis* ▶
**Length** 6 in (15 cm).
**Appearance** Adult head, nape and breast grey or grey-brown; upperparts rich brown with darker markings. Young birds browner and speckled.
**Distribution** Widespread resident in Britain and Europe, but summer only in north-east, and winter only in south-west.

Dunnocks used to be mistakenly called hedge sparrows, even though they have a slender, insect-eating beak, rather than a conical sparrow-type, seed-eating beak. They are widespread and often numerous throughout the year, being absent only from very exposed and treeless areas. Their choice of habitat is wide, and they are found in woodland, farmland, parks and gardens. In Britain and Ireland, dunnocks are familiar and usually tame garden birds, hopping about among the undergrowth and taking little notice of man, but on the Continent (perhaps as a result of persecution) they are extremely shy, living in deep cover. They lay up to six deep-blue eggs; two or more broods are normal.

## ICTERINE WARBLER *Hippolais icterina* ▶
**Length** 5 in (13 cm).
**Appearance** Upperparts greenish-grey, with yellow stripe over eye; underparts yellow; beak yellowish, relatively long and stout. Legs bluish.
**Distribution** Summer visitor to north, north-east and central Europe.

Icterine warblers inhabit the undergrowth of woods, parks and gardens, and also dense farmland hedgerows, and breed from northern France north-eastwards to Scandinavia, Poland and Russia. *Hippolais* warblers have a more upright stance than *Phylloscopus* leaf warblers, and have a long, low head profile which is often dramatically altered if the crown feathers are raised in excitement. Icterine warblers are scarce in Britain and Ireland, but occur at migration times annually, and are usually seen at bird observatories. The nest contains up to six deep pinkish eggs with dark brown spots.

**MELODIOUS WARBLER** *Hippolais polyglotta* ▶
**Length** 5 in (13 cm).
**Appearance** Greenish-olive above, yellow below; yellowish stripe above the eye; crown feathers sometimes raised; beak stout, relatively long; legs brownish-blue.
**Distribution** Summer visitor to south and south-west Europe.

Birds of open woodland undergrowth, gardens and parks, melodious warblers are summer visitors to southern Europe, breeding as far north as central France. In Britain and Ireland they are scarce, though regular, passage migrants, most birds being seen at bird observatories. Very similar to the more northerly icterine warbler (*H. icterina*), melodious warblers have shorter wings which barely reach the base of the tail when folded, whereas the icterine warbler's wings extend half way along the tail. Melodious warblers lay up to six deep pinkish eggs with dark brown spots.

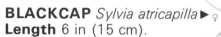

**BLACKCAP** *Sylvia atricapilla* ▶ ♀
**Length** 6 in (15 cm).
**Appearance** Upperparts grey-brown, darker on wings and tail; underparts pale grey, washed with buff; crown black in males, chestnut in females, brown in young; legs bluish.
**Distribution** Common, widespread summer visitor throughout Europe (including Britain); resident in the south-west.

Blackcaps breed primarily in deciduous woodland, becoming less common the further west and north you travel, and are occasional migrants elsewhere. Blackcaps have a rich, fluty song – a mellow warble that increases in intensity and volume and often ends on a high note. They sing from deep in cover, but tend to prefer a woodland habitat with both a reasonable amount of undergrowth and a substantial array of mature trees. Blackcaps now overwinter increasingly in the milder areas of western Europe, particularly in those parts of Britain and Ireland with an oceanic, rather than Continental, pattern of winter climate, often visiting feeding tables in gardens. Normally up to five pale brown eggs with darker markings are laid, and there are often two broods.

◀ **GARDEN WARBLER** *Sylvia borin*
**Length** 6 in (15 cm).
**Appearance** Nondescript; upperparts greyish-brown, tinged with olive; underparts white, shaded grey or grey-buff; legs bluish.
**Distribution** Widespread summer visitor to Britain and Europe.

One of the few birds with almost no noteworthy plumage characteristics, garden warblers are widespread in the deciduous woodlands of England and Wales, penetrating lowland Scotland but scarcer in Ireland than the blackcap. Their habitat preference is slightly, but significantly, different from that of the blackcap in that they demand plentiful undergrowth and scrub but seem to require no tall trees. The song is musical, mellow and liquid, sometimes rivalling that of the nightingale for quality, and it has the typical 'chack' alarm note of _Sylvia_ warblers. Usually up to five whitish eggs, sparsely speckled with brown are laid. In the south there are occasionally two broods.

## WHITETHROAT _Sylvia communis_ ▶
**Length** 6 in (15 cm).
**Appearance** Adult males have grey head, brown back, chestnut wings and a dark brown tail edged with white; underparts white, tinged buffish pink on breast. Females and young birds browner above, duskier below.
**Distribution** Widespread summer visitor to Britain and Europe.

Until the late 1960s, whitethroats were one of the most numerous and widespread of summer migrants to western Europe, breeding in scrub, on heaths and in open woodland and farm hedges. They have been slow to recover from a massive decline which occurred between the autumn departure in 1968 and the spring arrival of 1969, thought to have been caused by food shortage during an extended drought in their wintering quarters in the Sahel region of West Africa. Populations wintering further east in Africa (and breeding further east in Europe) seem to have escaped. Only now is the scratchy song of the whitethroat, produced in a jerky song flight above the scrub, beginning to be heard on anything like the old scale. The nest contains up to five yellowish eggs with dark spots, and there are usually two broods.

## LESSER WHITETHROAT _Sylvia curruca_ ▶
**Length** 6 in (15 cm).
**Appearance** Grey-brown above, with black patch through the eye; faint chestnut-brown on wings; tail dark brown, with a white edge; underparts white, shading to pinkish buff on the flanks.
**Distribution** Widespread summer visitor to Europe (including Britain), except for the south-west.

Lesser whitethroats breed in hedgerows, woodland undergrowth and scrub, laying up to six yellow-brown spotted eggs, sometimes in two clutches. Unlike many migrant warblers, which head south to Africa through Spain on a southerly course, lesser whitethroats head for their winter quarters in the Sudan on a south-easterly bearing through Italy. Even more unusual, they perform a 'loop migration', as their return path in spring is to the east of the Mediterranean before turning west and passing north of the Alps. Because of their different winter quarters, lesser whitethroats escaped the tragedy that overcame the whitethroat, when a drought severely reduced their numbers.

### WILLOW WARBLER *Phylloscopus trochilus* ▶
**Length** 4 in (10 cm).
**Appearance** Adults pale olive-green above, with whitish eye-stripe; off-white shaded yellow below; legs usually orange-yellow. Young birds have more yellow plumage.
**Distribution** Widespread summer visitor to central, eastern, western and northern Europe (including Britain).

Willow warblers are among the most abundant and widespread summer visitors to the woodlands of Europe. Their song, a silvery, descending trill is an annual indication that spring has truly arrived.

Willow warblers are not restricted in their choice of habitat, but prefer open woodland and scrub. Up to seven pale pink eggs with faint reddish freckling are laid, normally in a single clutch.

### CHIFFCHAFF *Phylloscopus collybita* ▶
**Length** 4 in (10 cm).
**Appearance** Adults brownish-olive above, with buff eye-stripe; off-white, buff-shaded below; legs usually blackish. Young birds have much richer buffs and yellow shading beneath wings.
**Distribution** Widespread European summer visitor (including Britain); resident in the south and south-east.

On sight, it is hard to distinguish chiffchaffs from willow warblers (*P. trochilus*), as leg coloration is not a reliable characteristic. Once they sing, however, there can be no mistake, since chiffchaffs repeat their name, sometimes stumbling over the order of the syllables, with monotonous regularity.

Most chiffchaffs are summer visitors to British and European woodlands, preferring mature trees. An increasing number now overwinter, especially in the milder west, and often visit gardens in search of additional food. Up to six white eggs with purplish spots are laid, and there is often a second brood.

### WOOD WARBLER *Phylloscopus sibilatrix* ▶
**Length** 5 in (13 cm).
**Appearance** Olive-green above, with yellow face; throat and breast contrasting with striking white belly; legs yellowish-brown.
**Distribution** Summer visitor to central, northern and north-western Europe (including Britain).

Wood warblers are birds of mature deciduous woodland; often oak or beech. Despite their bright colours and striking, accelerating trill of a song, they are surprisingly well camouflaged against the yellowish spring leaves as they flit about the canopy. One of the later summer migrants to arrive, wood warblers usually build a domed nest in the leaf litter of the woodland floor. They lay up to seven white eggs with heavy purple speckles, normally in a single clutch.

**BONELLI'S WARBLER** _Phylloscopus bonelli_ ▶
**Length** 4 in (10 cm).
**Appearance** Tiny; upperparts greenish-olive, rump strikingly yellow; underparts a characteristic silvery-white; legs brownish.
**Distribution** Summer visitor to south, south-west and central Europe.

Bonnelli's warblers are summer migrants to upland Mediterranean woodland breeding grounds, having overwintered in Africa. They breed as far north as central France, and it is probably overshooting spring migrants or wind-blown dispersing young that are responsible for the annual but occasional

records of this species in Britain and Ireland. Most sightings are at the coastal bird observatories. Up to six white, lavender-speckled eggs are laid.

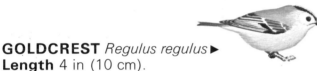

**GOLDCREST** _Regulus regulus_ ▶
**Length** 4 in (10 cm).
**Appearance** Tiny; adults olive-green above; brown tail and brown wings with double white wing-bars; pale ring round eye; crown with black-edged yellow stripe, and a crimson centre in the male; underparts whitish.
**Distribution** Widespread resident in many parts of Britain and Europe; winters only in the extreme south west.

Goldcrests share with firecrests (_R. ignicapillus_) the distinction of being the smallest birds in Britain and Ireland, weighing only about 5 grams. Although they are characteristic of coniferous woodland, after a series of mild winters numbers will be high and

goldcrests become plentiful in deciduous woods also, where during the breeding season their high pitched 'deedly-deedly-dee . . .' song will ring through the trees. They suffer severely during harsh winters, but fortunately numbers quickly recover. Goldcrests lay up to eight minute, white eggs, finely peppered with brown. There are two broods.

**FIRECREST** _Regulus ignicapillus_ ▶
**Length** 4 in (10 cm).
**Appearance** Olive-green above, with dark brown tail and dark brown wings with double white wing-bars; head pattern striking, with black-bordered orange crown and bold white stripe over the eye; underparts whitish.
**Distribution** Resident over much of west, south-west, south and central Europe (including parts of Britain).

Firecrests take over at the southern fringe of the range of the goldcrest (_R. regulus_), and extend down to the shores of the Mediterranean. Over much of their range they prefer deciduous woods, but in

Britain several colonies have been established in conifers – the preferred habitat of the goldcrest! Distinguished from goldcrests by their head pattern and monotonous 'zi..zi..zi...' song, firecrests build similarly suspended, strong, hammock-like nests.

◀ **SPOTTED FLYCATCHER** *Muscicapa striata*
**Length** 6 in (15 cm).
**Appearance** Dull brown above, with dark-streaked crown; buff below with dark streaks on breast; they appear long-winged in flight and rather short-legged when perching.
**Distribution** Summer visitor to most parts of Britain and Europe.

As their name implies, spotted flycatchers feed almost exclusively on insects caught in flight. Normally they will have several observation perches in their woodland or garden territory, and from one of these they will dart out and catch the prey (often with an audible snap) before returning to the same lookout perch. On these perches, or whilst making their forays, spotted flycatchers draw attention to themselves by sharp 'zit' calls. They habitually flick their wings and tail restlessly while perched. Usually four or five greenish eggs with chestnut spots are laid, and there are two broods.

◀ **PIED FLYCATCHER** *Ficedula hypoleuca*
**Length** 5 in (13 cm).
**Appearance** Adult males white below, black above with white wing-bars and white margins to the tail. Females and young similarly patterned, but upperparts buffish brown, underparts smoky white.
**Distribution** Summer visitor to parts of south-west and western Europe; widespread in Britain and northern Europe.

Unlike spotted flycatchers (*Muscicapa striata*) pied flycatchers nest in holes and readily take to nestboxes. Detailed studies of nestbox colonies have shown that some males are polygamous, and manage to support two females, although the first is usually left to rear her own brood of nestlings unaided. Usually five to eight blue eggs are laid and occasionally there is a second brood. Again, unlike spotted flycatchers, which hardly have a recognizable song, pied flycatchers have a rather un-melodious jangle of notes.

**MISTLE THRUSH** *Turdus viscivorus* ▶
**Length** 11 in (28 cm).
**Appearance** Adults buff-brown above, with white-edged tail; whitish below with heavy brown blobs on breast. Young birds paler, with silvery feather margins.
**Distribution** Resident in Britain and much of Europe; summer visitor only in the north and north-east.

One of the earliest woodland birds to begin breeding, mistle thrushes are locally called the 'storm cock' because of their habit of choosing a tall tree as a song post and singing their simply phrased but melodious song into the teeth of a March gale. Mistle thrushes build bulky nests, often with untidy and conspicuous streamers of paper or plastic blowing around them. A clutch of up to five eggs is laid, bluish with fine reddish spots, and there are two broods. They rely on their aggression and harsh rattling calls to drive off predators like jays, weasels or owls, both birds of the pair diving repeatedly and occasionally striking the intruder's head.

**FIELDFARE** *Turdus pilaris* ▶
**Length** 10 in (25 cm).
**Appearance** Crown, nape and rump grey; mantle and wings rich russet brown; tail black; breast pale chestnut with brown spots, paling to white on belly.
**Distribution** Winter visitor to southern and western Europe (including Britain); resident central and parts of northern Europe; summer visitor to extreme north.

Most fieldfares breed among the forests, town parks and gardens of north and north-eastern Europe, although recently a few pairs have bred in Britain. In the winter months, vast flocks visit western and southern Europe, often roosting in woods, but they are primarily birds of farmland, feeding on worms and other invertebrates on the ground, and, while supplies last, gorging themselves on hawthorn berries and rose hips. Seen at close quarters fieldfares are among the most beautiful of birds, and as the winter weather harshens, many come into suburban gardens where they can be tempted by fallen apples, or sliced apples put out specially for them. Four or five pale blue-grey eggs with brownish freckles are laid.

75

**REDSTART** *Phoenicurus phoenicurus*
**Length** 6 in (15 cm).
**Appearance** Adult males with white forehead,
grey crown and mantle, brown wings and
chestnut tail; face and throat black; breast
chestnut. Females and young brown above, buff
below; tails chestnut.
**Distribution** Widespread summer visitor to
Britain and Europe.

Over much of Europe, redstarts are numerous
breeding birds in open deciduous or mixed
woodland, extending their range in some parts into
parks and large gardens. In the west, they seem to
prefer the damp oakwoods of hill country, and in the
north it is the birchwoods on the uplands that are
favoured. They are inexplicably absent from
Ireland, except as occasional passage migrants. It is
thought that their ancestral habitat was probably
old pinewood, but although redstarts will nest in a
variety of sites, including even pollarded streamside
willows, they do not seem to have colonized
extensive modern conifer plantations. Within their
woodland or parkland habitats they are hole-
nesters, using nestboxes, natural holes in trees or
cavities in dry stone walls or buildings, and disused
woodpecker excavations. Up to seven bluish eggs,
very rarely with darker spots are laid, and
sometimes there is a second brood.

**NIGHTINGALE ▶**
*Luscinia megarhynchos*
**Length** 7 in (18 cm).
**Appearance** Adults olive-brown above, with
chestnut on wings, and a long rich-rufous tail;
underparts buff. Young birds similar, but speckled
buff.
**Distribution** Summer visitor to most of Britain
and Europe.

The voice of the nightingale, often heard at dead of
night on the warm summer air, is one of the most
beautiful bird songs in the world. Part of the thrill in
listening to the nightingale's song, deep in its
deciduous woodland or scrub habitat, lies in its
sheer variety. The song ranges from throaty
chuckles to far-carrying whistles, and rich cello-like
phrases to the purest of treble trills. Nightingales
usually lay four or five bluish eggs, spotted with
brown. In Britain nightingales are restricted to
south-east England.

## BLUE TIT *Parus caeruleus* ▶
**Length** 5 in (13 cm).
**Appearance** Adults green-backed, with blue wings and tail; underparts yellow; head white, outlined in black, with black bib and line through the eye, and blue crown. Females slightly duller than males. Young greener, lacking black patterns.
**Distribution** Widespread resident throughout Britain and Europe, except for the far north.

Although primarily woodland birds, blue tits are catholic in both their choice of habitat and food selection. Most will be found in woodland during the winter, feeding acrobatically and often upside down on insect eggs hidden at the ends of the canopy twigs. Others will venture into gardens, where they are popular visitors to the bird feeding table, although they are less welcome when they attack the tops of milk bottles, pecking a hole in the foil through which they drink the cream. A few can even be found in reed-beds, seeking out insects overwintering in the reed stems. Up to 15 tiny brown-flecked white eggs are laid, and there is usually a single clutch.

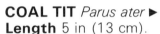

## COAL TIT *Parus ater* ▶
**Length** 5 in (13 cm).
**Appearance** Adults have olive-grey back, pale fawn beneath; head and bib black, with bold white cheek patch and white square patch on nape. Young birds drabber, lacking black markings.
**Distribution** Widespread resident throughout Britain and Europe.

Although they often occur in deciduous or mixed woodland at any time of year, coal tits are primarily birds of coniferous woodland, especially during the breeding season. They are as widely distributed across Britain and Ireland as the great and blue tits, but are nowhere as common, except in conifers. Like the other tits, they are regular garden visitors during the winter, with a particular liking for peanuts, flying to hide their food in a bark crevice or among the leaves of an evergreen such as the yew – a cache against possible scarcity later in the season. Up to 11 tiny red-speckled white eggs are laid, usually in a single clutch.

## CRESTED TIT *Parus cristatus* ▶
**Length** 5 in (13 cm).
**Appearance** Adults brown above, pale buff below; head white, with pattern of black lines and long chequered black-and-white crest. Young duller, lacking crest and bold markings.
**Distribution** Widespread European resident (including parts of Britain).

On the Continent of Europe, crested tits are both numerous and widespread in coniferous and mixed woodland. In Britain, they are rare birds confined to the Caledonian forest, an area of ancient conifers in the Highlands of Scotland. Sedentary birds, they manage to survive the Highland winter, often straying into gardens, before returning in the summer to nest in cavities in the old Scots pine trees, where they lay up to seven red-spotted white eggs.

**MARSH TIT** *Parus palustris* ▲
**Length** 5 in (13 cm).
**Appearance** Adults brown above, pale fawn below; glossy black cap contrasting with whitish cheeks; small black bib. Young birds drabber.
**Distribution** Widespread British and European resident except for the south-west and north.

Marsh tits are widespread throughout the year, and sometimes common in predominantly deciduous woodland with plentiful undergrowth. They are much scarcer from the level of the Baltic northwards, and absent from Ireland. This species and the willow tit (*P. montanus*) are very difficult to separate, but the call (marsh tits often use an explosive 'pit-chew') helps, as does the pale wing-patch which is normally visible in the closed wing of the willow tit. Up to eight tiny white eggs, faintly spotted with red are laid, usually in a single clutch.

**WILLOW TIT** *Parus montanus* ▶
**Length** 5 in (13 cm).
**Appearance** Adults brown above, pale below; dull black cap and black bib contrast with whitish cheeks; pale buff patch often visible as panel in centre of closed wing.
**Distribution** Resident throughout Britain and Europe, except for the south-west.

Willow tits are widely distributed year-round in all types of woodland, preferring damper areas. Although absent from Ireland, they have penetrated into Scotland and well north into Scandinavia and Russia, unlike marsh tits (*P. palustris*). Again, unlike marsh tits, which use natural cavities, usually in trees, willow tits excavate their own nest hole in soft or rotten timber. They therefore have more powerful neck muscles than their relative, which give them a characterisically bull-necked appearance and this, coupled with their 'dee dee' or 'chay' calls, may ease identification problems. Up to nine tiny white eggs, flecked with red, are laid in the nest hole.

**LONG-TAILED TIT** *Aegithalos caudatus* ▶
**Length** 6 in (15 cm).
**Appearance** Tiny body with long tail; upperparts a mixture of browns, pinks, and white; head white with black stripes over eyes; tail black, white edged; underparts white. Young birds browner than adults.
**Distribution** Widespread resident throughout Britain and Europe.

Long-tailed tits are probably more closely related to the tropical babbler family than to the true tits. Parties of long-tailed tits roam scrubby woodland, farmland and rough ground drawing attention to themselves by their continuous trilling calls, which help keep the flock together in dense cover. The nest is a domed woven masterpiece of hair, moss, lichens and feathers (over 2000 feathers have been counted in the lining), embedded deep in a thorny bush and flexible enough to accommodate the growing brood. Up to 12 minute white eggs, finely freckled with red are laid, and this species is single brooded.

**NUTHATCH** *Sitta europaea* ▶
**Length** 6 in (15 cm).
**Appearance** Adults and young woodpecker-like, grey above with black mark through eye and white patches on tips of tail feathers; underparts buff; chestnut flanks, richer and more extensive in males.
**Distribution** Widespread resident throughout Europe (including parts of Britain); absent from the far north.

Although woodpecker-like both in build and in many of their actions whilst seeking insects behind bark or hammering open a nut held in a regularly used crevice 'vice', nuthatches are unrelated to the woodpeckers. Unlike woodpeckers, they have normal soft tail feathers, and can move about sideways and head-down on the trunk, in contrast to the woodpeckers' inevitable head-up posture. Resident in mature open woodland and parks, nuthatches are hole-nesters, laying their eggs on a nest lining of flakes of bark and characteristically reducing the size of the entrance hole and plastering up cracks with mud. Up to nine white eggs are laid, heavily speckled with dark brown, in a single brood.

**TREECREEPER** *Certhia familiaris* ▶
**Length** 5 in (13 cm).
**Appearance** Upperparts brown, flecked white; underparts whitish; tail long, brown and rigid; beak long, finely pointed and down-curved.
**Distribution** Widespread resident in Britain and north, north-east and central Europe.

As their name implies, treecreepers spend much of their time on trunks and branches seeking insects and their eggs and larvae concealed in crevices. Although quite unrelated to the woodpecker family, they, too, have rigid and very strong central tail feathers which serve as a prop to support them as they spiral up trunks, always head-up, before gliding away to the base of another tree to begin again. They normally nest behind a loose flap of bark, laying up to six white eggs with dense brown speckles. There is often a second brood.

◀ **SHORT-TOED TREECREEPER**
*Certhia brachydactyla*
**Length** 5 in (13 cm).
**Appearance** Upperparts brown, flecked white; underparts whitish, often shading to buff on the flanks; beak long, finely pointed, down-curved.
**Distribution** Widespread resident of south, south-west and central Europe.

Short-toed treecreepers are similar to the tree-creeper (*C. familiaris*), but differing slightly in the measurement of the hind claw and in the colour of the flanks. Short-toed treecreepers are birds of Continental deciduous forests, treecreepers on the

Continent being birds primarily of conifers. Short-toed treecreepers are resident on the Channel Islands, but are extremely scarce vagrants to the east coast of mainland Britain. Up to six white eggs with reddish spots are laid.

♂ summer

**HAWFINCH** *Coccothraustes coccothraustes* ▶
**Length** 7 in (18 cm).
**Appearance** Underparts pinkish beige; upperparts rich brown, with grey collar and blackish-purple wings; crown chestnut, beak massive, triangular and silver-grey; conspicuous double white wing-bar and short white-tipped tail in flight. Young drabber and more speckled.
**Distribution** Widespread British and European resident, except for the north.

Although they are the largest of the British finches, hawfinches are so secretive in their habits that they are suprisingly rarely seen. They spend much time in the treetops, and if they do drop to the ground, it is only after a cautious wait to see if it is safe to do so. They are widely if irregularly distributed in woods and on farms. Wild cherries, sloes, horn beam, beech and cultivated damsons are among their favourite foods, and the massive beak, powered by strong muscles (hence the relatively large head), is said to be capable of exerting pressures of 200 pounds per square inch (14 kg per cm²) to crush the seeds or stones, and extract the nutritious kernel within. Hawfinches lay up to six bluish eggs with dark squiggles; there is normally only one brood.

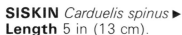

**SISKIN** *Carduelis spinus* ▶
**Length** 5 in (13 cm).
**Appearance** Males green, streaked with black above; black crown and bib; yellow rump and tail patches; underparts streaky-yellow shading to white. Females and young browner, heavily streaked.
**Distribution** Resident throughout Britain, northern and eastern Europe; winter visitor to southern Europe.

At one time siskins were typically birds of conifer woodland in the west and north of Europe during the breeding season, relatively few venturing to the south-west in winter to feed upon the cones of stream-side alders. With increasing numbers of conifer plantations and with alders being planted as windbreaks in the orchards of areas such as south-eastern England, the siskin is now flourishing, increasing in both range and numbers. Recently, too, these shy woodland birds have taken to visiting garden bird tables, particularly attracted to orange plastic net containing peanuts. The normal clutch-size is of up to six bluish eggs with brown spots and there are two broods.

81

**REDPOLL** *Acanthis flammea* ▶▶
**Length** 5 in (13 cm).
**Appearance** Adults buff, heavily streaked with brown above; paler, often pinkish and less streaked below; whitish beak, small black bib and small red patch on crown. Young lack crown and bib patches.
**Distribution** Resident in Britain and northern Europe; winter visitor to central Europe.

Redpolls are birds of birchwoods. They are widespread, and on the increase as breeding birds, having adapted to most types of woodland. Now few woods in summer do not have a male circling high overhead, trilling in an almost continuous twitter. In winter, where they were once birds of riverside alders in the lowlands, redpolls are again becoming far more widespread. Some will feed in alder windbreaks in orchard country, but many others join with other finches and buntings in feeding on weedy stubble, pastures and rough ground. Redpolls lay up to six brown-spotted, bluish eggs and there are sometimes two broods.

**SERIN** *Serinus serinus* ▶
**Length** 4 in (10 cm).
**Appearance** A small finch; dark-streaked olive-green above, with a striking yellow rump; dark-streaked yellow shading to white below. Females and young duller, with less yellow.
**Distribution** Resident in southern Europe; summer visitor to central Europe.

On the Continent serins are widespread in parks, gardens and open woodland, particularly towards the Mediterranean basin. A few migrants reach Britain – usually south-east England – each year, and in recent years a small number has remained to breed in good summers in southern counties. Serins lay up to five pale blue eggs with purple-brown spots and streaks.

**BULLFINCH** *Pyrrhula pyrrhula* ▶
**Length** 6 in (15 cm).
**Appearance** Both sexes have a dark cap, dark wings and tail; bold white rump-patch conspicuous in flight; beak finch-like, rounded in profile, black. Males grey above, rich pink below. Females a mixture of buff-browns. Juveniles resemble females but lack the black cap.
**Distribution** Widespread British and European resident.

On record as a pest, eating buds from fruit trees in winter, bullfinches are secretive birds favouring the dense cover of scrub and woodland margins, leaving them to attack gardens and orchards. The plaintive whistle that keeps the pair in contact is often heard, but the quiet creaking song only rarely. The nest is a flat twiggy platform, the cup lined with hair, usually in a thorny bush. Two broods, each of four to six bluish eggs with dark brown spots and squiggles are usual. Bullfinches are widespread, often common birds, rarely moving more than a few miles in Britain, although they are often migratory in northern Europe.

### ◄ CROSSBILL *Loxia curvirostra*
**Length** 7 in (18 cm).
**Appearance** Adult males dark crimson with brown wings and tail; females yellowish-bodied. Young birds buff-bodied with many dark streaks. Beak bulky, crossed at tip.
**Distribution** Patchily distributed across Britain and Europe.

The flattened, cross-tipped beak of crossbills is adapted to extract the seeds from between the rigid woody segments of conifer cones. The size of the beak varies between crossbill species and races, the small-billed two-barred crossbill tackling soft larch cones, the crossbill eating spruce, and the heavy-beaked parrot crossbill capable of dealing with the biggest cones of pine. Continental crossbills occasionally 'invade' eastern England and remain to breed there for a year or two, but in the Scottish Highlands some crossbills (taxonomists debate whether these are parrot or Scottish pine crossbills), reside year-round in the Caledonian Forest.

### ◄ CHAFFINCH *Fringilla coelebs*
**Length** 6 in (15 cm).
**Appearance** Males have pink breast, rufous back, grey head (with black forehead) and dark wings with bold white wing-bars. Females and young various shades of beige, but with white wing-bars.
**Distribution** British and European resident; summer visitor only in the north-east.

Chaffinches are numerous birds of woodland, farmland and parks and gardens. In Britain, censuses have shown that the chaffinch is a contender for the title 'most numerous bird', particularly during the winter when resident birds are joined by huge numbers from the Continent. With their descending cascade of song, with a final flourish, ringing through the trees in early spring, chaffinches are popular birds, adept at begging crumbs from picnickers. The lichen-covered nest is neat and extremely well concealed and unusually for a finch, one brood of four or five pale blue, brown-smudged eggs is the norm – perhaps a tribute to the quality of the camouflage.

**BRAMBLING** *Fringilla montifringilla* ▶
**Length** 6 in (15 cm).
**Appearance** Summer males have black head
and back, white rump, orange breast shading to
white and dark wings with orange and white
bars. Females, young and winter males duller, but
with traces of orange and conspicuous white
rump.
**Distribution** Widespread British and European
winter visitor; breeds in the extreme north of
Europe.

Brambling numbers fluctuate widely from year to
year, and in some areas roosting flocks millions of
birds strong have been recorded. Although some
stay late into the spring in southern Europe, and
there have been reports of breeding, bramblings are
predominantly winter visitors to the greater part of
the Continent. It seems that in most areas, it is the
quantity of beech seed, or mast, that determines
brambling numbers, and most beech trees set heavy
seed crops in alternate years. In winters when there
is little beech mast, or in areas where beech is
scarce, a few bramblings may be seen, with
chaffinches, feeding in the fields. Up to seven dark
greenish eggs with purple-brown spots are laid.

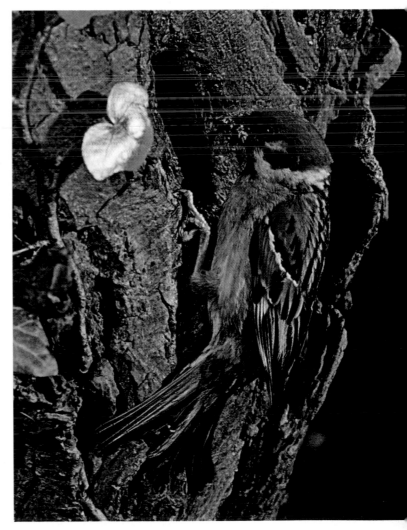

**TREE SPARROW** *Passer montanus* ▶
**Length** 5 in (13 cm).
**Appearance** Both sexes and young mottled
brown above, with chestnut crown, black patch
in the centre of white cheeks, and black bib;
underparts white.
**Distribution** Widespread British and European
resident.

Very much 'country cousins' to the house sparrow,
tree sparrows tend to be much shyer and to shun
man and his buildings. However, they often use
ruined or deserted buildings in which to build their
bulky grass nests, and will readily occupy
nestboxes (often put up for other birds) in
woodland. They are gregarious and robust, and
despite their relatively small size will quickly evict
even great tits, promptly filling the nestbox with
straw and feathers and laying on top of the
unfortunate tit's eggs or young. Four to six dull
white eggs, speckled with grey or brown, are laid,
and there are up to three broods.

# Downland and man-made habitats

Although the most artificial of the European habitats, these environments have become important sanctuaries for many birds. Gardens and hedgerow-linked copses have become, in effect, woodland edges in their own right. In addition, the regular sowing and ploughing of farmland provide ample food for many opportunist species.

The clearances in the extensive forest cover of the past were not, of course, carried out solely to provide timber for domestic fuel, housing, ships or, more recently, industrial fuel. They were in fact an essential part of an expanded agricultural industry, aiming both to feed the growing population and at exploiting export markets. The process of clearance produced, almost as an incidental consequence, a much more varied landscape than the original forests.

Initially, the clearances would have been small and widely scattered, but since medieval times they have extended and coalesced to produce today a network of copses and woodlands, linked by a still extensive (though diminishing) series of hedgerows. (Even the pattern of hedgerows has waxed and waned, with changing farming practice dictating first large clearances and then the enclosures, at which time many present-day hedges were probably planted.) Within this overall system crops are also grown, of course, and agricultural land now covers much of the landscape. The system of linked woods and hedgerows forms both a means of communication and a reservoir for wildlife which can then exploit adjacent farmland.

It is interesting to reflect on the impact of these forest clearances. It seems likely that the net effect has been a beneficial one, although there may well have been some reductions or even losses – notably of larger species like the goshawk or the honey buzzard, which demand extensive forest areas for breeding. Overall, it seems very probable that many of the farmland species of today were originally birds of the forest margins. Clearances for agriculture would have enhanced the opportunities afforded to many, or most, of these by vastly increasing the amount of 'forest edge', thus providing more space for nesting territories and more extensive, and diverse, feeding habitats.

## DOWNLAND

Downland as it occurs today is also largely the product of agriculture, being formed from clearances in the woodland cover on which animals, mostly sheep, were fed. The grazing pressure from the sheep, and from rabbits – for which this newly created habitat was ideal – prevented the growth of most trees and shrubs, resulting in the typical downland scene of wide expanses of grassland, often steeply sloping, studded with the occasional hawthorn bush.

A number of birds are typical of this habitat: the ever-present skylark, for example, and in many areas the equally dowdy-looking meadow pipit. Wheatears prefer the closely grazed areas, occasionally nesting in disused rabbit burrows, while whinchats are more often seen where the grass is longer. Whinchats require a perch from which to scan for their insect food on the ground, as does the red-backed shrike, another summer migrant from Africa. The red-backed shrike is also known as the 'butcher-bird' from its habit of impaling its prey (beetles, bees, worms, small rodents and birds) on hawthorn spikes for later consumption. In winter, true downland is rather devoid of birds, although the great grey shrike may occasionally overwinter there, and the skylarks often remain, too.

## FARMLAND

Farmland also has some characteristic birds. These include the two species of partridge: the common and the red-legged. Regrettably the increasingly widespread techniques of modern farming are reducing the food supply of the common partridge considerably, and this once common game bird is now becoming rather rare in some areas. The more strikingly coloured red-legged or French partridge is holding its own rather better. Another game bird, the pheasant, long ago imported from the Far East, is a handsome addition to European open countryside. The coppery body, bottle-green head, and very long tail feathers are shown off to best effect as the pheasant struts across the ploughed field or stubble.

Even if naturalists had not already considered the skylark to be almost the emblem of farmland, poets and song writers certainly have. Singing whilst hovering high over its midfield territory and nest, the skylark is entirely characteristic of this type of habitat. It sings from early spring to late autumn

1 robin (*Erithacus rubecula*)
2 kestrel (*Falco tinnunculus*)
3 swift (*Apus apus*)
4 house martin
   (*Delichon urbica*)
5 pheasant
   (*Phasianus colchicus*)
6 skylark (*Alauda arvensis*)
7 black-headed gull
   (*Larus ridibundus*)
8 blackbird (*Turdus merula*)
9 goldfinch (*Carduelis carduelis*)
10 red-backed shrike
   (*Lanius collurio*)
11 common partridge
   (*Perdix perdix*)
12 great tit (*Parus major*)

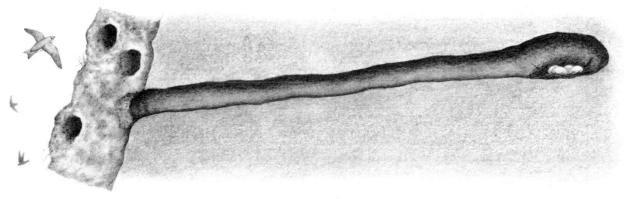

and even occasionally on fine, warm winter days.

The kestrel, Europe's commonest bird of prey, can sometimes also be seen over fields, and sometimes over town parks, rough ground or roadside verges. The old country name for this species is 'windhover', and indeed the bird is master of the art of hanging stationary in the air, watching for the movement of a vole or a mouse – or even a large beetle – sometimes 100 ft (30 m) or more below. Most predatory birds are equipped with exceptionally good eyesight, and often also with very well-developed hearing. This is especially true of the owl family, which do much of their hunting at dusk or during the night, when acute sight is of less value. The barn owl, once common over farmland, has become a rare bird, although there are some signs of a recovery. As its name implies it nests in farm buildings, especially deserted or semi-ruined ones. Fortunately it is generally looked on with favour by the farmer, as it contributes to the management of farmland by taking a proportion of rats and house mice among its prey. The little owl, with its characteristic yelping call, is another farmland bird. A smaller bird, streaked grey-brown with white spots, it lacks the heart-shaped face of the barn owl, and features far more insects in its diet. Despite only having an overall length of 8–9 in (20–23 cm), it will tackle and kill birds as big as blackbirds or mistle thrushes to feed to its young, which are normally reared in a hollow in a tree.

Most farmland birds have a wide-ranging diet, and seem able to adapt quickly to new foods. The crow family in general exemplify this, and none better than the magpie. The magpie's diet is composed largely of small soil animals such as worms and various insects and their larvae, augmented by carrion, cereal seeds, fruit, berries and even the occasional unwary lizard, frog or small mouse. They extend their search for insects by seeking out the fly maggots and ticks which live in the fleece of sheep, and will often use a sheep's back as a convenient vantage point to scan the grass for insects. Magpies range over most farmland, showing some preference for rough grazing fields with thick

Man's building activities have been beneficial to species such as the sand martin, which burrows out nest holes in sandy cliffs. Many colonies can now be found in the artificial cliff faces of commercial sand quarries.

unkempt hedges, and taller trees suitable for building their football-sized domed nests of prickly twigs. They tend to avoid prairie farmland and treeless marshes, and shun equally tracts of dense woodland without any clearings.

During the autumn and winter months, large flocks of birds gather on the fields. Often these are house and tree sparrows, linnets, chaffinches, greenfinches, yellowhammers or skylarks feeding on weed seeds left after crop harvesting, but also large flocks of rooks, jackdaws, lapwings and gulls gather to feed on worms, insect larvae, or just to rest. Gulls are now so much a feature of inland countryside, following the plough to gather worms from freshly overturned clods or feeding widely scattered across meadows, that it is difficult to realize that this habit for birds so typically associated with the sea has only developed since the early years of this century. At that time the black-headed gull – now a regular visitor to town parks and lakes – was a great rarity inland.

Of all farmland's man-made habitats, it is the hedgerows that are probably the most valuable to bird populations, as they provide a place to nest and a source of both food and shelter at all times of the year. The birds that frequent them are much the same as the species seen in gardens – blackbirds, thrushes, robins, wrens and dunnocks, for example – but in areas of arable or cereal farming species like the handsome yellowhammer, with its bold yellow and black head, or the very drab buff corn bunting, may be seen. Of the summer visitors, the white-throat is probably the most characteristic.

There are, sadly, obvious examples where man has exerted too much influence on this mosaic of fields, woods, copses and hedgerows. Perhaps in most cases the cause has been too great a pursuit of high profitability or productivity, although each of these must be among the legitimate goals for any farmer. The swing of the pendulum that enclosed with hedges the huge fields of a few hundred years ago has been reversed, and in some areas expanses of uniformity have reappeared, this time as the 'prairie farmlands' of extensive cereal monoculture. With the vital spinneys and hedgerows gone, and with an intensive spray programme of pesticides and herbicides reducing not just pest insects but almost all species, and not just weeds but almost all wild plants to drastically low levels, such areas become almost uninhabitable by birds.

## URBAN ENVIRONMENTS

If hedges are considered as extensions of well-gladed woodland penetrating into open farmland, then gardens and parks, particularly in country towns or in the older-established suburbs, can also be considered as green tendrils, penetrating the brick and concrete of built-up areas. A large number of birds has proved versatile and adaptable enough to exploit these green areas, although they are almost totally man-made and contain a majority of completely alien garden plants, shrubs and trees.

They also contain rich and fascinating opportunities for close-range birdwatching; although many of the birds involved may be classed as common, they all exhibit extremely good adaptations for their co-existence with man. Because of this, the birdwatcher can enjoy the privilege of watching them go about their daily lives with little difficulty – even from an armchair! The provision of food plants in the garden, nestboxes or regularly feeding the birds in winter will obviously add to the range of birds to be seen, and thus to the enjoyment.

Tits, various thrushes and finches, the robin, dunnock and wren all come to mind as familiar garden birds. Some – particularly the house sparrow and starling – are well able to survive in the concrete canyons of the inner city, and the smallest of city squares, with just a few bushes and trees, will encourage blackbirds and woodpigeons. The tawny owl and kestrel can also survive here, and are successful city-centre birds, living on mice and sparrows, nesting in tree holes or nestboxes, or on the substitute 'cliff ledges' of old churches. The kestrel even nests on the window sills of high-rise flats.

Carrion crows have been recorded breeding on St

Birds, especially tits, are quick to exploit unusual foods put out for them in the garden.

Paul's Cathedral in the centre of London, and with its omnivorous habits, which include secretive early-morning visits to garden bird tables and scavenging on town rubbish tips, the magpie has also shown itself well able to adapt to modern town life. Moreover, it is demonstrating the speed at which novel feeding techniques can spread through bird populations. The best-known example of this is the way in which blue and great tits open milk bottles, but now magpies are demonstrating similar opportunism by following milkmen on their early morning rounds. They have learned to relate the milk float to deliveries of one of their favoured foods – eggs. No matter that the eggs arrive neatly packaged in cartons on the doorstep: the cartons are equally easily recognized and soon opened by the strong beak and the contents greedily eaten!

### ◄ KESTREL *Falco tinnunculus*
**Length** 14 in (35 cm).
**Appearance** Adult males have grey head with black moustache; back chestnut spotted with brown; tail grey with black band; underparts buff streaked with brown. Females larger: brown, barred-black above; tail brown with numerous dark bars. Young resemble females.
**Distribution** Widespread throughout Britain and Europe.

The commonest and most widespread of the falcons, kestrels are at home on hills, moorland, farmland and woodland fringes, and have successfully colonized many towns, where an ample supply of mice and house sparrows is available as food, and where window ledges on high-rise blocks of flats substitute adequately for the natural cliff-ledges usually used for nesting. They lay up to six pale eggs, spotted with red. Even the wide expanses of motorways and their verges have proved ideal terrain for the kestrel's characteristic hovering hunting technique.

### GREY OR COMMON PARTRIDGE►
*Perdix perdix*
**Length** 12 in (30 cm).
**Appearance** Adults are dumpy, often with an upright stance; face chestnut; breast and nape vermiculated grey; back mottled brown; brown bars on grey flanks. Dark chestnut horseshoe-shaped patch on belly more prominent in male. Young birds nondescript buff.
**Distribution** Resident throughout Britain and Europe, apart from the south-west.

Partridges are easily recognized by their dumpy shape when seen on grassy or ploughed fields, although their habitat also extends on to the margins of the moorland territory more properly the home of the red grouse. The nest, in which are laid nine to twenty olive-brown eggs, is exceedingly well concealed in the base of a tussock, and as a further predator-avoidance stratagem, the young can fly when less than half-grown. This presents a fascinating spectacle if a hen and her brood are disturbed and they whirr away, bullet-like, on stiff, often down-curved wings. In many areas, increasingly sophisticated farming techniques – and especially the use of cereal insecticides which eliminate a vital food supply for the young – seem to be causing a steady decline in partridge numbers.

◀ **PHEASANT** *Phasianus colchicus*
**Length** Males 34 in (85 cm);
females 23 in (58 cm).
**Appearance** Males unmistakeable, with long
black-barred tail, iridescent bronze-coloured body
and green head with scarlet fleshy face patches.
Females well camouflaged in sandy buffs and
browns. Young resemble females.
**Distribution** Resident throughout most of
Britain and Europe, excluding the south-west.

Pheasants, now so widespread in the agricultural
lowlands but less numerous elsewhere, were
introduced to Europe from China many centuries
ago. They were present in Britain around the time of
the Norman conquest, and may well have been
imported in Roman times. In many parts, numbers
are maintained by regular releases of large numbers
of captive-reared birds for sporting purposes, and it
may well be that the 'patchwork quilt' of field and
woodland that is so rich in wildlife owes its
continued existence to the shooting syndicates and
large estates which maintain it as 'good pheasant
country'. Pheasants lay 12 or more buff brown eggs.

◀ **CORNCRAKE** *Crex crex*
**Length** 11 in (28 cm).
**Appearance** Adults mottled brown above, with
grey throat and chestnut-barred flanks;
conspicuous chestnut patch on wing visible even
when closed. Young birds paler and buffer.
**Distribution** Widespread summer visitor;
winters in south-west Europe.

The scientific name for the corncrake highlights
their rasping 'crex-crex' call as one of the best
identification features, for they are secretive birds
which demand long periods of cautious and silent
observation to obtain a good view. Because of
increased farm mechanization, with the mower
replacing the scythe and the ever-earlier havesting
of grass crops both for silage and hay, corncrakes
are rapidly declining birds. In Britain and Ireland,
only a few hundred pairs of this summer migrant
remain, centred in western Ireland and on the
Western Isles of Scotland, where suitable long-
grass areas are not cut until late in the season. They
lay eight to twelve greenish, brown-spotted eggs.

92

**LAPWING** *Vanellus vanellus* ▶
**Length** 12 in (30 cm).
**Appearance** Adults unmistakeable, with pied plumage, chestnut under-tail feathers and long fine crest; beak short. Juveniles similar, but lack green sheen to black feathers many of which have buff margins.
**Distribution** Resident in much of Britain and Europe; winters in south-west Europe.

Lapwings are waders, and so can be expected to be found primarily in coastal habitats. Most will breed in marshy areas – some near the coast, some inland – but at other times of the year, lapwings may be seen on all types of open fields, including dry stubble, freshly ploughed fields and flooded grassland. Usually four olive-brown eggs are laid. The name lapwing refers to their 'floppy' flight, emphasized by the flickering of black-and-white plumage. Their alternative name, peewit, accurately reflects their wild rasping call.

pale subspecies

**BARN OWL** *Tyto alba* ▶
**Length** 14 in (35 cm).
**Appearance** Pale chestnut above, flecked brown-and-white; white below; heart-shaped facial disc white; eyes dark. Long, white-feathered legs.
**Distribution** Resident in most parts of Britain and Europe.

Evening or night-time hunters, barn owls present a ghostly appearance as they glide by in the moonlight, on silent wings. The apparition is made all the more startling by the owl's eerie shrieking call. Barn owls prey heavily on small rodents, and are a useful element in farmyard biological control. Fortunately many farmers recognize their value, and put up nestboxes in secluded corners of new barns to replace old nest sites when traditional barns are demolished and old hollow trees are removed from hedgerows. Equally fortunately, barn owls are quick to accept these replacement homes. Up to seven round, white eggs are laid; often two broods are produced.

**COLLARED DOVE** *Streptopelia decaocto* ▶
**Length** 11 in (28 cm).
**Appearance** Sandy-brown above, paler and pinker below; wings brown; tail brown with broad white margins; black-and-white collar extending around nape.
**Distribution** Resident throughout Britain and much of Europe.

Until the mid-1950s, although widespread on the Continent, collared doves had not been recorded in Britain and Ireland, but the success story from then until the present day is one of the most remarkable of any bird. Asian in origin, collared doves started a westward spread in the 1930s. The precise cause is unknown, but was perhaps due to a genetic mutation. In 1955 the first pair bred in Norfolk, rapidly followed by others in south-east England. A decade later, collared doves had increased to such an extent that they were classed as pests of stored cereals and chicken farms in some areas and by the 1970s, they were breeding even in western Ireland and the Outer Hebrides. They do not appear, surprisingly, to have displaced other species in the process. The nest contains up to three glossy eggs, and several clutches can be produced at any time.

◀ **LITTLE OWL** *Athene noctua*
**Length** 9 in (23 cm).
**Appearance** Upperparts brown, spotted with white; underparts off-white streaked with brown; facial disc greyish; darker patches around the eyes and with striking pale 'eyebrows'.
**Distribution** Resident in Britain and Europe.

Now widespread throughout the year in open woodland and farmland – and even in some parts on coastal cliffs and islands – in England and Wales, little owls are scarce in the Scottish lowlands and absent from Ireland. Birds of the Mediterranean area, little owls owe their presence in Britain to a series of introductions during the 19th century. Although they often catch small rodents and birds (even up to the size of a mistle thrush), little owls eat many insects and worms. The nest contains five white eggs, laid in a single clutch.

94

**CRESTED LARK** _Galerida cristata_ ▶
**Length** 7 in (18 cm).
**Appearance** Streaked with brown and fawn above, pale fawn below with dark streaks on upper breast. Conspicuous crest, often held erect.
**Distribution** Widespread European resident; very scarce in Britain.

For birds which are so common and widespread year-round throughout Europe, there are astonishingly few records of crested larks in Britain, almost all confined to the south-east corner where the sea crossing is the shortest. Characteristic calls – usually a 'dee-dee-doo' – the short dark tail with pale chestnut outer feathers, and the long crest all help separate the crested larks from skylarks. Both species live in open country with short vegetation, but crested larks in particular frequent roadside verges. The nest contains up to five glossy, off-white eggs boldly marked with lavender.

**SKYLARK** _Alauda arvensis_ ▶
**Length** 7 in (18 cm).
**Appearance** Adults streaked brown above, on flanks and on breast; creamy below; tail dark with white outer tail-feathers. Juveniles paler and more scaly. Small crest inconspicuous except when alarmed. Walks along ground; rarely hops.
**Distribution** Widespread British and European resident.

Skylarks are best known for their delightfully musical territorial song, a continuous series of chirps, twitters, trills and whistles, usually delivered during the high, hovering songflight of the male, but occasionally from a post or the ground.

Skylarks breed in open farmland and grassland, from sand dunes to high altitude moors, but tend to congregate in lowland areas in winter, and may form flocks several hundred birds strong. When snow covers the seeds and invertebrates that make up their main diet, or when these become scarce in spring, skylarks may cause considerable damage to brassicas and seedling sugar-beet. Many are forced to migrate south or west to escape the cold. Three or four greyish, brown-spotted eggs are laid.

### SWALLOW *Hirundo rustica* ▶
**Length** 8 in (20 cm).
**Appearance** A slender, graceful bird, dark blue above except for red 'face' and white spots on tail; underparts white or pinkish; tail forked: adults more than juveniles, and males more than females.
**Distribution** Widespread British and European summer visitor.

Airborne insects caught in a characteristic grass or water-skimming flight, and up to great heights, form the sole diet of both adult and young swallows. Apart from a few nests attached to trees, cliffs and in caves, their robust feather-lined, mud and straw nests are always placed on a ledge in man-made sites, especially farm outhouses and garages. Four or five white eggs, reddish-brown spotted, are laid, and successive broods are reared in the same nest, and these may all return to roost together at night. In autumn vast numbers congregate to roost in reed-beds, and then migrate over the Sahara to South Africa, returning in late March and April to breed throughout most of Europe. Red-rumped swallows (*Hirundo daurica*), are scarce visitors to Britain and Ireland, and build their house martin-like nests in Spain and around the Mediterranean.

### ◀ HOUSE MARTIN *Delichon urbica*
**Length** 5 in (13 cm).
**Appearance** Agile, rather dumpy aerial-feeder with slender wings and forked tail; upperparts blue-black except for conspicuous white rump; from below, dark wings and tail contrast with white body. Young birds resemble adults.
**Distribution** Widespread British and European summer visitors.

House martins typically catch their insect prey at higher levels than swallows but, like swallows, they land to collect damp mud in their bills for their half-cup shaped nest, in which are laid four or five white eggs. Even in city centres, artificial nests under suitably wide eaves attract house martins, and nests of adjacents pairs often touch. Although second clutches are laid only a week after the first brood has flown, long incubation and fledging periods mean that second broods rarely fly before mid-September and that some third broods can still be found in October. House martins often gather on telegraph wires especially prior to migration, their white-feathered feet and legs being easily visible. British and Irish birds are thought to winter in South Africa, but their habits are not well known.

## SAND MARTIN *Riparia riparia* ▶
**Length** 5 in (13 cm).
**Appearance** Smallest European hirundine; more slender than house martin; tail only slightly forked; upperparts, wings and tail earth-brown in colour, white underparts with narrow inconspicuous brown band across chest. Juveniles have pale feather fringes on upperparts.
**Distribution** Widespread British and European summer visitor.

Sand martins are one of the earliest summer visitors to arrive in Britain and Europe, the first birds appearing in Britain in mid-March, usually over lakes and reservoirs, where they catch most of their insect prey. Recent sand and gravel excavation has provided this species with an abundance of safe, though sometimes noisy, breeding sites in addition to their more natural riverbank haunts. Both sexes scrape at the soil with their tiny feet to form a tunnel up to 4 ft (1.3 m) deep, and catch feathers and wisps of grass in flight for the terminal nest chamber, in which are laid four or five white eggs. Some sand-martin colonies are sited in stone walls and embankments, where drainage pipes are used as nests. Young birds often visit other colonies, even several hundred miles away, before migrating.

## MEADOW PIPIT *Anthus pratensis* ▶
**Length** 6 in (15 cm).
**Appearance** Adults and young are brown above with some darker markings; paler below, with streaked brown-black breast and flanks; outer tail-feathers white; legs brown.
**Distribution** Resident throughout north and north-west Europe (including Britain); winter visitor to south and south-west Europe.

Meadow pipits thrive in open country, breeding in rough, sheep-grazed grassland, sand dunes, downs and moors, and moving to lowland areas in winter. Their squeaky alarm and flight call – 'tsiip' – and trilling, parachute-like song flight are often the only sounds of bird life on high moors. Meadow pipits are characteristically active and, as their fine bill suggests, feed almost solely on insects. The nest, built of grasses and lined with hair, is carefully hidden among tussocky grass, but this gives little protection from the cuckoo which, in Britain, has a distinct preference for the nests of this species. Meadow pipits lay four or five eggs, which are usually mottled or marbled brown or grey, but may be pale grey or pale blue.

97

**GREAT GREY SHRIKE** *Lanius excubitor* ▶
**Length** 10 in (25 cm)
**Appearance** Large, boldly marked bird with
long, rounded tail and stout hooked beak;
underparts whitish; upperparts grey; tail black
with white outline; wings black with white bars;
mask black. Females duller. Young birds
brownish-grey above with some crescent-shaped
marks below.
**Distribution** Widespread European resident;
winter visitor to Britain.

Great grey shrikes are the largest and most
formidable of the European shrikes, their hawk-like
beaks being well adapted for tearing prey such as
small birds, mammals, frogs, lizards and large
insects. Although widely distributed throughout the
northern hemisphere, including all but the north
coast of France, they are only scarce autumn and
winter visitors to eastern Britain. Such migrants
arrive from October onwards, mostly from Scandinavia, and often return to the same feeding
territories in successive years. The superficially
similar lesser grey shrike (*L. minor*) is smaller, with
a shorter tail, black forehead and less white on the
wings. From its comparatively restricted breeding
range, this species migrates to Africa, displaced
individuals occurring annually in Britain in spring
and autumn. The nest contains up to six off-white
eggs, densely speckled with browns and greys.

◀ **RED-BACKED SHRIKE** *Lanius collurio* ♀
**Length** 7 in (18 cm).
**Appearance** Wings and back of males chestnut;
crown, nape and rump grey; black plumage
confined to mask and white-bordered tail.
Females browner and duller, without facial
markings, and scaly below. Juveniles lack grey
coloration, and scales prominent both above and
below.
**Distribution** Summer visitor to many parts of
Britain and Europe.

For no clear reason, red-backed shrikes have been
declining throughout Britain and Western Europe
for at least a century. The recent cooler, wetter
summers may have reduced the numbers of
grasshoppers, mantises, beetles, dragonflies, bees,
moths and butterflies which they eat, but other
factors are probably also involved. Egg-collecting
has also been implicated, for the great variation in
colour of red-backed shrike eggs – brown, greenish
and even white – made them popular, but this is
probably only significant locally. The few pairs that
do return from Africa each May choose dry
heathland habitats with a mixture of gorse, small
trees and heather, and lay five or six eggs. Here, like
other shrikes, they store their surplus food in
larders, impaled on thorns or barbed wire.

Hooded crow

## CARRION/HOODED CROW *Corvus corone* ▶
**Length** 18 in (45 cm).
**Appearance** Carrion crow: all-black; stout black beak with bristles at base; 'thigh' feathers smooth. Hooded crow: black head, wings and tail; body grey. Hybrids with intermediate plumages occur.
**Distribution** Carrion crow resident in west, central and south-west Europe, and Britain); Hooded crow resident in north, east and south east Europe, and western Britain.

Hooded or grey crows (*C. c. cornix*) are scavengers with a marked taste for game bird eggs and sheep carrion in the hills, while carrion crows (*C. c. corone*) share this liking for eggs but obtain most of their carrion from urban refuse tips. Carrion crows have adapted extremely well to urban life, and may even nest in city centres. Usually four to six glossy, pale blue-green, dark spotted eggs are laid.

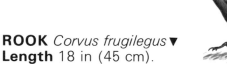

## ROOK *Corvus frugilegus* ▼
**Length** 18 in (45 cm).
**Appearance** Males, females and juveniles black with glossy metallic sheen; dagger like beak; feathers of the upper leg are loose and rough, giving a 'baggy trousered' appearance, and this, together with the call – a raucous 'carr' – helps distinguish rooks from carrion crows.
**Distribution** Resident in many parts of Britain and Europe; winters also in the south.

Early in spring, rooks may be seen in spectacular and noisy aerial display flights over their rookery, a colony of nests ranging in size from a dozen or so to a few hundred, usually built high in the tallest trees around. Six greenish eggs are laid, heavily speckled with brown. Rooks spend most of their time feeding on meadows or arable farmland, and breed early so that the young may be raised successfully on a diet of small soil-dwelling animals before the ground becomes too dry and hard for their probing beak to penetrate. Adults have a pouch for carrying food back to the nest, visible as bare-skinned white cheek patches, in contrast to young birds, which have black bristles at the base of the beak.

juv.

**JACKDAW** *Corvus monedula* ▲
**Length** 13 in (33 cm).
**Appearance** Head and body dark, variable amount of grey on nape and upper breast, most conspicuous in adults early in the breeding season; striking white eye.
**Distribution** Resident in most parts of Britain and Europe except extreme north.

Jackdaws are widespread residents of woodland and farmland. On farmland they eat many soil pests, but undo this good by taking freshly sown seed, particularly peas. They nest in hollows in trees, or in cavities in the towers of churches or other little-used or deserted buildings, but will sometimes build a bulky twig nest in a house chimney, causing a great deal of trouble when the first fire of the autumn is lit. Up to six pale, blue-green eggs with brown spots and streaks are laid.

**STARLING** *Sturnus vulgaris* ▼
**Length** 9 in (23 cm).
**Appearance** Adults blackish, with greenish and purplish sheens, faintly spotted with buff or white in summer, heavily spotted in winter; beak black in winter, yellow in summer, blue at base in males, pink in females. Young birds grey-brown, darker above than below.
**Distribution** Widespread resident in Britain and Europe.

The summer breeding population of starlings on western European farmland, woodland and urban areas is greatly augmented during the winter months by many millions of migrants from further north and east of the Continent. These, and local birds, feed on damp grassland and fallen orchard fruit, gathering to roost in immense flocks, which fill the sunset sky like clouds of black smoke. Many of these roosting flocks crowd on to buildings in city centres — seeking the extra warmth provided by central heating — but others gather in woodland, where their acidic droppings may form a layer several centimetres deep, destroying all the vegetation. Usually four to seven pale blue eggs are laid, and there are one or two broods.

**MAGPIE** *Pica pica* ▲
**Length** 18 in (45 cm).
**Appearance** Adults unmistakeable, with black-and-white body and wings and long black tail with greenish iridescent sheen. Young birds have shorter tails.
**Distribution** Resident throughout Britain and Europe.

The nest is a conspicuous, bulky, football-sized sphere of thorny twigs, usually built high in a tree or deep in an equally thorny bush, into which up to seven heavily mottled, greenish eggs are laid. Magpies occasionally show the habit of 'stealing' bright objects and taking them to the nest — which has given rise to the 'thieving magpie' legends. This behaviour has not yet been fully explained — it may be that they are seeking nest ornaments, or that it is just inquisitive behaviour. So inquisitive are they, and such arch egg-thieves, that in some towns even doorstep deliveries of eggs in cartons are robbed.

## SONG THRUSH *Turdus philomelos* ▲
**Length** 9 in (23 cm).
**Appearance** Brown above, tinged yellowish-buff; chestnut in wings and tail; whitish below, tinged with pale chestnut, bold brown spots on the breast.
**Distribution** Resident in Britain and western Europe, wintering in the extreme south-west; summer visitor to north and north-east Europe.

Song thrushes can be found in woods, parks, gardens and farmland. Their song, varied and flute-like, is melodious but repetitive. A unique feature of song thrushes is their habit of eating snails, a food source exploited by few other birds. Once caught, the snails are taken to a regularly used stone or hard path (known as a 'thrushes' anvil') and smashed open. Song thrushes usually lay four or five blue eggs with a few blackish spots, and there are two or three broods.

## REDWING *Turdus iliacus* ▶
**Length** 8 in (20 cm).
**Appearance** Dark russet-brown above, with white eye-stripe and moustachial streak; underparts whitish, streaked with brown, shading to rich russet on the flanks.
**Distribution** Summer visitor to north and north-east Europe, winter visitor to the rest of Europe (including Britain).

Redwings are common breeding birds in Scandinavian and other northern birchwoods, parks and gardens, and are winter visitors to the rest of Europe. Some winter visitors to the western fringe of Europe may be slightly larger and darker, and originate from Icelandic breeding stock. Most winter redwings feed in fields and orchards during the day, roosting in woodland at night. In recent years their range has extended southwards, and a few pairs have stayed on to breed in Britain, so the simple series of flute-like notes that constitutes their song is now becoming as familiar as their thin 'tseep' flight call is on a late autumn night. Up to seven greenish, brown-freckled eggs are laid.

**BLACKBIRD** _Turdus merula_ ▶
**Length** 10 in (25 cm).
**Appearance** Adult males velvet-black, with orange beak and eye-ring. Female russet-backed, browner beneath, sometimes with dark-bordered pale throat. Young paler than female and buff-spotted.
**Distribution** Resident throughout Briatin and Europe, except for the far north.

An attractive feature of blackbirds is the way they live cheerfully and successfully in towns, even though they seem to fall prey depressingly often to cats or, under the pressures of dashing about to find adequate worms to feed their youngsters, fly fatally in front of cars. They have strident alarm calls, and are aggressive in defence of their territory: neighbouring males, each puffed up to present an intimidating appearance, will pace up and down for hours along opposite sides of the imaginary line separating their territories. The clutch of up to five bluish eggs are finely peppered with pale brown spots. Usually there are two or three broods, but five have been recorded!

**ROBIN** _Erithacus rubecula_ ▶
**Length** 5 in (13 cm).
**Appearance** Adults sandy-brown above; breast red, grey-fringed. Young birds speckled brown all over.
**Distribution** Widespread resident throughout Britain and Europe; summer visitor to the north-east.

A conspicuous feature of Christmas cards, the robin has a special charm, not least from its habit of following gardeners in the hope of some freshly dug worms. In winter, both sexes are territorial, but in spring the female's hormones repress her aggression and the male reacts to this by allowing her into his territory. Robins lay up to seven whitish eggs, finely freckled with reddish-brown and there are usually at least two broods. Robins have always been at the centre of superstition: to kill one was regarded as sacrilege, a feeling perpetuated in the nursery rhyme 'Who killed cock Robin?' Such beliefs stem from the fable that the robin attempted to remove Christ's crown of thorns — receiving for its efforts a drop of blood, carried ever after as the red bib.

**Distribution** Widespread British and European resident, except for the north.

Widespread throughout most of Britain and Ireland except for north-west Scotland, greenfinches are typical birds of hedgerows, parks, gardens and woodland fringes and clearings. Duller in winter, and often tending to feed on the ground where they seek fallen seeds, in summer the male displays over his territory. Flying high in a series of loops, he beats his wings in a slow-motion 'butterfly' flight; the flight-song is a twittering, purring trill. In gardens, greenfinches are regular bird-table visitors. They lay up to six eggs, sparsely streaked with brown; usually in two clutches.

**GREENFINCH** *Chloris chloris* ▲
**Length** 6 in (15 cm).
**Appearance** Adult males olive-green above, yellower below; bright yellow patches on wings and tail; grey on the head. Females drabber olive-green. Young browner and more streaked.

imm.

**GOLDFINCH** *Carduelis carduelis* ▶
**Length** 5 in (13 cm).
**Appearance** Adults have brown back, white rump, black tail, and black wings with bright gold wing-bar; underparts buff fading to white; black nape, white head with scarlet face patch. Young birds have the wing-bar, but are otherwise pale streaky buff.
**Distribution** Widespread British and European resident.

The collective name for a group of goldfinches is a 'charm', which sums up their attractive appearance, particularly when seen as a flock feeding on autumn thistle heads or teasels. Their beaks are longer and more finely pointed than those of most finches: well adapted for extracting seeds from such prickly surroundings. They lay up to six bluish eggs with darker squiggles and there are usually two broods. Many goldfinches are found on farmland, heaths, commons and other rough ground with plentiful weed cover. Others migrate, however, and because of their attractive appearance and twittering song may be caught for caging by Continental trappers.

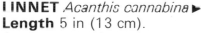

**LINNET** *Acanthis cannabina* ▶
**Length** 5 in (13 cm).
**Appearance** Summer males chestnut-backed, with pale rump and white-edged black tail; head and underparts pale fawn, with pink crown and breast. Females, young and winter males browner, lacking pink.
**Distribution** Resident throughout most parts of Britain and Europe; summer visitor to the north and north-east.

Linnets are often common along farm hedges, on heaths and commons, woodland fringes and weedy waste ground. They often nest in loose colonies, and the males are an attractive sight, particularly if their chosen song-post, as often happens, is a gorse bush in full flower. Up to six bluish eggs with dark squiggles are laid, and there are two or three broods. In their drabber winter plumage they are well camouflaged when feeding on the ground, looking for weed seeds on ploughed land, stubbles and coastal marshes. In south-eastern England, some have developed a taste for the seeds of strawberries, even entering the polythene tunnel cloches under which the earliest crops are grown!

### ◄ GREAT TIT *Parus major*
**Length** 6 in (15 cm).
**Appearance** Adult males greenish above, yellow below; black crown and nape contrasting with white cheek patch; black bib extending to broad stripe down centre of breast and belly. Females duller, black stripe much less defined. Young greener, without the black markings.
**Distribution** Widespread resident throughout Britain and Europe, except for the far north.

The largest of the British and Irish tits, great tits often feed on the ground, even when in flocks with other tits, using their stouter beak to feed on fallen seeds and nuts as well as insects. Although both their calls and song (most often a repetitive 'tee-cher tee-cher') are simple in structure, great tits possess one of the most comprehensive ranges of calls of any bird, with 90 or more variations on record. Although they are mainly woodland birds they have adapted readily to life along farmland hedgerows and gardens. Great tits usually lay up to 12 red-spotted white eggs in a single clutch.

### ◄ CORN BUNTING *Emberiza calandra*
**Length** 7 in (18 cm).
**Appearance** Adults and young plump; drab fawn, streaked with dark brown; wedge-shaped beak.
**Distribution** Resident in most parts of Britain and Europe, except northern Europe.

Corn buntings are dumpy looking birds which are predominantly residents of open land such as heaths, downs and extensive grass or cereal fields. In Britain they are most numerous in eastern England and Scotland, although in all places discontinuities in distribution are sometimes difficult to explain. The plumage must rate among the least distinguished of any bird, but such is the harsh nature of the corn bunting's song that the birds are very noticeable in their open habitat. Uttered from a prominent place – a post or telephone wire – the song has been likened to shaking broken glass in a tin, or jangling a bunch of keys. The nest contains between three and five pale buff eggs with blackish squiggles.

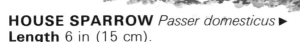

## HOUSE SPARROW *Passer domesticus* ▶
**Length** 6 in (15 cm).
**Appearance** Males rich mottled-brown above; grey crown and chestnut nape; bib black, underparts otherwise drab white. Females and young mottled-brown above, fawn below.
**Distribution** Common and widespread British and European resident.

Wherever there is evidence of man in the form of crops or buildings, even in the most remote areas, colonies of house sparrows will be found. They are among the most widespread and numerous of British and European birds year-round, having adapted so well to living in built-up areas that the majority of their food is produced by man, and most of their nest sites are holes in buildings. Three to six pale eggs, speckled with grey, are laid and there may be as many as four broods. In some large factories and major railway stations, the house sparrow population never ventures into the open air, depending on man's scraps for food. In rural areas, they can do considerable damage to cereal crops.

## ORTOLAN BUNTING *Emberiza hortulana* ▶
**Length** 6 in (15 cm).
**Appearance** Males have brown back with dark streaks, head olive-grey, with pale throat and distinct whitish eye-ring; underparts dull cinnamon. Females and young similar, but paler and drabber.
**Distribution** European summer visitor except for the west; occasional migrant to Britain.

Ortolan buntings have a breeding range extending from the Mediterranean north to Sweden and Finland, but with a predominantly eastern European bias. They are summer visitors, wintering in Africa, and all that we see of them in Britain and Ireland is an annual trickle of records of stray migrants, in spring and autumn, mostly trapped for ringing at the bird observatories. They are considered a gastronomic delicacy in France. Between four and six off-white eggs, speckled and streaked purple brown, are laid.

## CIRL BUNTING ▶
*Emberiza cirlus*
**Length** 6 in (15 cm).
**Appearance** Adult males upperparts chestnut; rump olive; crown dark with black streak through the eye; underparts yellow; bold black throat and greenish collar. Females and young streaked brown; buff below; rump olive.
**Distribution** Resident in south, south-west and central Europe; a few are found in southern Britain.

Cirl buntings are primarily birds of Mediterranean scrub or *maquis*, and it is thought that subtle climatic changes may be responsible for their decline in Britain, where they are now restricted to a few patches of downland in the southern counties. Although female cirl buntings and yellowhammers (*E. citrinella*) are very similar, the males have both a distinctive plumage and distinctly different songs; that of the cirl buntings is little more than a dry metallic rattle on a single note. Cirl buntings lay three to five bluish eggs with dark squiggles and blotches, and there are two broods.

# Rivers, lakes and marshes

From tranquil, reed-fringed lowland lakes to the rushing torrents of winter-swollen upland streams, the freshwater habitats of Britain and Europe are among the most important of all for birds. Whether as permanent homes, migratory staging posts or chance feeding sites, this environment attracts species from many different orders.

Rivers, lakes and marshes are collectively known as wetlands, a term which also embraces a number of other predominantly freshwater habitats such as bogs, swamps, reed-beds and water-meadows.

Many types of wetland are among the most ancient natural features of the countryside. This is particularly true in remoter areas where the influence of man is likely to have been less. More recent man-made freshwater habitats have also been adopted quickly by many birds, and these include canals, reservoirs, sewage treatment works and flooded or semi-flooded mineral workings. These may range from sand, marl and chalk pits, through to the sand and ballast workings and clay pits more usually associated with the flood plains of river valleys.

Within this extremely broad band of habitats are found widely varying conditions, ranging from those of nutrient-rich lowland lakes and rivers to those of oligotrophic upland lakes where the nature of the rock, together with the harsher climate, result in fewer, more specialized types of birds. These differences in conditions are reflected overall by an enormous diversity of bird species, each adapted to exploit the prevailing conditions.

## BIRDS OF UPLAND FRESH WATER

Upland lakes in the far north and north-west attract two fascinating birds groups in particular. One of these groups is the waders, and perhaps the most interesting European representative is the red-necked phalarope. This bird has some distinct and unusual characteristics. The female is larger and

1 swift (*Apus apus*)
2 grey heron (*Ardea cinerea*)
3 common tern
   (*Sterna hirundo*)
4 marsh harrier
   (*Circus aeruginosus*)
5 kingfisher (*Alcedo atthis*)
6 sand martin (*Riparia riparia*)
7 coot (*Fulica atra*)
8 tufted duck (*Aythya fuligula*)
9 great crested grebe
   (*Podiceps cristatus*)
10 redshank (*Tringa totanus*)
11 bearded tit
   (*Panurus biarmicus*)

more brightly coloured than the male, and dominates display. Having laid a clutch of eggs, she departs, leaving the male to incubate them and raise the brood while she seeks a fresh mate, thus maximizing her productivity. Phalaropes also have a fascinating feeding habit: they spin round on the surface of shallow lakes, and the vortex created stirs up food items from the bottom.

The other family of birds associated with upland lakes is the divers. Both red-throated and black-throated divers breed annually (not all divers do this), and are among the most spectacularly handsome of birds. Their song, too, is remarkable. In America this bird family are called loons, supposedly because of the similarity of their song to uncontrolled maniacal laughter. Perhaps more likely is that it is derived from the Icelandic *lomr*, meaning lame, reflecting these waterbirds' extreme clumsiness on land.

Some upland lakes flow down to the sea, often in the form of fast-moving streams. When these contain fishes such as salmon and trout they provide food for a variety of birds, including the 'sawbill' ducks: the goosander and red-breasted merganser. The long, narrow beaks of these birds are specialized for feeding on fish, having a serrated edge and hooked tip well suited to catching their slippery prey. But how is it that two similar species share the same habitat? As is usual in such cases, there are subtle differences that help the two to co-exist without competition: for instance, the goosander lives and breeds further inland and at higher altitudes, while the red-breasted merganser stays near the coast.

Three smaller birds also characterize fast-moving streams and, although they are unrelated, they share the same habit of bobbing up and down continuously. The smallest and brightest of the three is the grey wagtail – a bird usually seen at waterfalls, weirs and mill-races on more sluggish streams – and the largest is the common sandpiper. Perhaps the bobbing habits of these birds help to conceal them against a background of moving, sparkling water.

The third bird associated with upland streams is the dipper. This bird is a relative of the thrushes, and is most unusual as it often feeds under water, searching for insect larvae. This bird may swim in quite deep water, using its wings in slow-motion 'flight', before bobbing up again and perching, tail cocked like a huge wren, white belly prominent, on a favoured boulder.

## BIRDS OF LOWLAND FRESH WATER

The slower-moving and often muddier streams in the lowlands, usually meandering through a flat

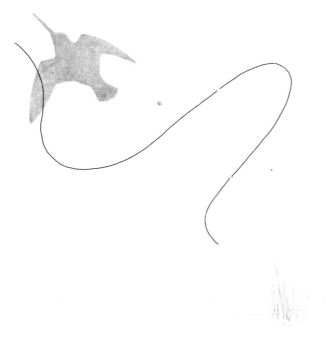

When flushed from cover, the snipe rises steeply, zig-zagging as it does so. (The related jack snipe flies off in a shorter, looped pattern.)

countryside, are sometimes less productive for birdwatching, but on occasions do offer more than the 'routine' sightings of mallard, moorhen and mute swan. In many parts, these are the year-round hunting grounds of the kingfisher. In winter, the alders that often line the banks of such rivers and streams provide food, in the form of their cones, for two small, acrobatic, but delightful finches, the redpoll and the siskin.

A change in our attitude to the wearing of bird feathers, coupled with an increase in suitable habitats, led to a recovery in the much reduced population of the great crested grebe around the turn of the century. These beautiful birds are at their best in the spring, when their fascinating courtship 'dance' on the surface of the water can be closely watched.

On some of the larger and deeper stretches of water the birdwatcher may also be lucky enough in winter to see the red-necked, the black-necked or the Slavonian grebe. At the same time of year reservoirs may also play host to the goosander and red-breasted merganser. In most years they are joined by small numbers of a third sawbill, the smew from arctic Russia. During the winter months many normally estuarine ducks may be found in the more hospitable freshwater areas well inland. These include 'dabbling' ducks like mallard, wigeon, teal, shoveler and pintail; and the usually smaller, rather dumpy 'diving' ducks, like the tufted duck and pochard. The mute swan occurs on many types of waters and is now often joined by the Canada goose.

Also typical in the same habitats are moorhens and coot.

Many older-established inland waters are accompanied by areas of marshy vegetation, and often by extensive reed-beds. In autumn these may be used as a roosting site by starlings, sand martins and yellow or pied wagtails, but in summer they are the main breeding area for several attractive small birds such as the reed bunting and the sedge warbler. In some areas the bittern breeds. This bird, a relative of the heron, is seldom seen but is often heard 'booming' – its call is a distant, foghorn-like sound. Also found in these reed-fringed freshwater habitats is the bearded tit, and the skulking water rail.

In late summer muddy edges may be exposed on many freshwater areas, and it is always worthwhile to scan the new shoreline for visiting waders on return passage from their breeding grounds. In many towns sewage disposal is still by largely non-chemical means, and a visit to the local sewage farm is always worthwhile. In these farms treated sewage is allowed to settle in sludge beds, and surplus treated liquids are often spread on a nearby field. Both these processes produce food-rich mud or shallow pools with lush grassy surroundings much visited by snipe and, later in the year, by teal. Many of the so-called 'marsh' waders – sandpipers for example – have established regular spring and autumn migration routes, passing through inland sewage farms, ballast pits or reservoirs.

One of the most skilful of avian builders, the reed warbler weaves its nest around reed stems.

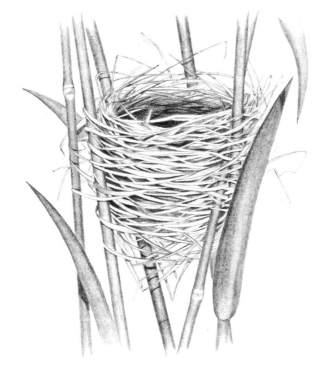

summer

▲
**GREAT CRESTED GREBE** *Podiceps cristatus*
**Length** 18 in (45 cm).
**Appearance** Adults in summer are grey-brown
above and white below; best identified by their
long neck, prominent dark chestnut ear-tufts and
crest, and dagger-like orange-yellow beak; in
flight appears hump-backed, showing bold white
wing patches. In winter, head ornamentation is
lost. The small young are striped black and white;
older young resemble winter adults.
**Distribution** Resident throughout most of
Britain and Europe.

From near extinction at the hands of the millinery
trade, great crested grebes have recovered to their
current healthy state, breeding on large expanses of
fresh water. In part this recovery stems from the first
bird protection legislation in the 1870s, but it is also
due, paradoxically, to the industrial activities of
man. The reed-fringed 'lakes' created by flooding
derelict mineral extraction workings (like sand and
ballast pits) greatly increased the area of favourable
habitat available. The grebes found them ideal for
building their floating nests and for their elaborate
courtship 'dance', when, rearing up in the water, the
male presents the female with a frond of waterweed.
Usually four or five chalky white eggs are produced;
occasionally two broods. Many inland waters also
hold great crested grebes in winter, but others move
to shallow, sheltered coastal bays and estuaries.

## LITTLE GREBE _Podiceps ruficollis_ ▼◄
**Length** 10 in (25 cm).
**Appearance** Adults in summer are dark brown, diminutive and with a 'tail-less' appearance; throat dark chestnut; small yellow patch at base of beak. Winter adults brown above, paler below. Small young striped; older birds resemble winter adults.
**Distribution** Resident throughout most of Britain and Europe.

Little grebes, or dabchicks, are common and widespread along slow-moving rivers, canals and streams, marshland ditches and dykes, and on lakes; in fact, in any heavily vegetated freshwater habitat. In dense reeds the grebes' high-pitched whinnying call may be heard in summer more often than the birds are seen, as they will submerge at the first sign of danger, sometimes just leaving their head above water. The floating, raft-like nest of decaying vegetation is 'moored' to nearby reeds so that it rises and falls with the water level, averting flooding. Up to six chalky white eggs are laid in two or three clutches. Some little grebes remain on fresh waters in winter; others can be seen on sheltered coastal seas.

## GREY HERON _Ardea cinerea_ ▲
**Length** 36 in (90 cm).
**Appearance** Adults grey above, underparts white; long slender white neck; head white with black streak through the eye continuing into a drooping crest; beak large, yellowish and dagger-shaped; legs long, yellowish. Young birds resemble adults but lack crest. In flight, herons flap their wings in a ponderous fashion, the head sunk between the shoulders.
**Distribution** Resident throughout most of Britain and Europe.

Herons resort to wetlands of all descriptions (including sheltered sea coasts in winter) in search of their food. Their staple diet of fish is supplemented by eels and frogs, together with any unwary snakes, water voles and ducklings. They have even been known to take water rails and dabchicks that come too close as they stand, motionless, waiting for prey. Most herons nest in woods, building substantial structures – often 3 ft (1 m) across – of large twigs high in the branches. Into this they lay up to five small, chalky-blue eggs. Others may nest in reed-beds, and in some areas they may be solitary, rather than gathered in sizeable heronries. During display, and when feeding their young, their harsh 'frank' call is uttered along with noisy shrieks and gurgles.

113

**PURPLE HERON** *Ardea purpurea* ▶
**Length** 31 in (78 cm).
**Appearance** Adults dark grey-brown above, dark chestnut to black below; long thin neck is chestnut with black streaks; legs are long and brown; beak long, dagger-shaped and yellowish. Young birds sandy-brown above, paler below.
**Distribution** Summer visitor to southern Europe.

Purple herons are rare visitors to Britain and Ireland, usually favouring freshwater marshes, lakes and ditches with dense vegetation, similar to the reed-beds where they nest in colonies (sometimes with other herons and egrets) in their Continental breeding areas. The nest contains up to five pale blue-green eggs. Purple herons appear considerably smaller, slimmer and darker than grey herons (*A. cinerea*), with less contrast in flight between the grey wings and black flight feathers, but with a more bulging neck and considerably larger feet, the long hind claw being held upright.

◀ **NIGHT HERON**
*Nycticorax nycticorax*
**Length** 24 in (60 cm).
**Appearance** Adults have blackish backs, grey wings and black crowns; underparts white; beak black; legs yellowish. Young birds streaked brown, boldly spotted white on back and wings.
**Distribution** Summer visitor to southern Europe.

Genuinely wild night herons only occasionally wander to Britain and Ireland. They are birds of freshwater marshes and swamps of southern Europe, feeding on various water animals. Mainly birds of the tropics, they share this habitat with other small herons and help to avoid competition for limited food resources by roosting during the day and feeding in the evening – the reverse of the normal pattern. They lay up to five blue-green eggs, and occasionally there are two clutches. A small colony of these birds, originating as escapes, breeds in the grounds of Edinburgh Zoo.

### ◄ BITTERN *Botaurus stellaris*
**Length** 30 in (75 cm).
**Appearance** Adults brown and heron-like, with plumage a mixture of buffs and browns streaked with black; crown dark; throat white; beak yellowish; legs greenish. Young birds resemble adults.
**Distribution** Resident throughout most of Britain and Europe.

Only rarely are bitterns seen in flight over the extensive reed-beds that are their home throughout the year. In the air, they resemble brown versions of the grey heron (*Ardea cinerea*), but with more rounded wings. In the reed-beds the plumage comes into its own for camouflage purposes, however, for when alarmed, bitterns 'freeze', head and neck erect, body slimmed, so that the black streaks run vertically and the birds merge superbly with the reed stems behind them. Bitterns are skulking birds, often solitary and often hunting food in the fading light of evening. Their diet consists mainly of frogs, but includes all sorts of water animals from newts and dragonfly larvae up to the nestlings of other waterbirds. Their presence would often go undetected were it not for their peculiar, booming call. Up to seven olive-brown eggs are laid.

### WHITE STORK *Ciconia ciconia* ►
**Length** 40 in (100 cm).
**Appearance** Adults dirty white above and below, with black flight feathers; neck long with a long dagger-shaped red beak; long red legs. Young birds resemble adults but have brown beaks and legs.
**Distribution** Summer visitor to Spain and parts of northern Europe.

Rare but annual visitors to Britain and Ireland, they are seen in small numbers each year on marshes, wet meadows and on dry grazing land. Lizards and grasshoppers feature often in their diet, along with frogs and fish. Most records are of birds blown off-course during spring and autumn migration periods, but occasionally birds are seen during the summer months. In flight, storks can be distinguished from herons not just by their black-and-white plumage, but because they fly with head and neck outstretched. White storks lay up to five white eggs, in a single clutch.

### ◄ SPOONBILL *Platalea leucorodia*
**Length** 34 in (83 cm).
**Appearance** Adults white; egret-like but with a long spoon-shaped black beak with yellow tip; loose white head crest in breeding season. Young birds similar, but lacking crest and with pinkish beak and black flight feathers.
**Distribution** Scarce summer visitor to Holland and Spain; more numerous in extreme south-east Europe.

At close range the spoon-shaped beak makes the spoonbill unmistakeable as it sweeps through shallow water seeking small fish, crustaceans and molluscs. Spoonbills breed in reed-beds beside extensive areas of fresh or brackish water, building bulky platforms of old vegetation among the reeds on to which they lay up to six white eggs with red spots and streaks. Although still rare visitors on migration away from their breeding areas, there are increasing occurrences of spoonbills spending the summer months on suitable wetland habitats in eastern England. The signs are hopeful that after an absence of a century or more, recolonization will take place and a successful colony of breeding birds, similar to that in Holland, may soon become established.

### ◄ GREATER FLAMINGO
*Phoenicopterus ruber*
**Length** 50 in (125 cm).
**Appearance** Unmistakeable; enormously long neck and legs; down-curved banana-shaped beak. Adults body small, plumage pale pink; wings scarlet and black. Young birds smaller, greyish, gradually acquiring adult plumage.
**Distribution** Resident in parts of Spain and southern France.

So successfully do the various flamingo species breed in captivity that the vast majority of those seen in the wild in northern Europe are probably escapes from waterfowl collections. Most are not even of this species, which breeds in southern France and Spain. Even so, these escaped birds are spectacularly colourful, and their feeding technique is fascinating to watch, with head upside-down and beak submerged in water or mud. Fine plates like whalebone inside the beak filter out small animals or algae from the water. The small, chalky white egg is incubated in a curious nest of mud.

**MUTE SWAN** *Cygnus olor* ▶
**Length** 60 in (150 cm).
**Appearance** Adults white; neck long and serpent-like, beak orange with black knob. Young birds grey-buff.
**Distribution** Resident in Britain and northern Europe.

There are few sights more impressive (or more alarming) than an adult male mute swan, wings raised over his back like a miniature galleon in full sail, swimming across the water in powerful surges towards an intruder threatening his nest – be that intruder a fox or an interested human being with no thoughts of ill intent. They are just as impressive as they power past in flight, their wing feathers creaking audibly under the strain of their enormous weight – they are the world's heaviest flying birds. Mute swans are found on all types of fresh water – and occasionally in sheltered coastal waters – and have adapted well even to the lakes in town centre parks. They are often seen grazing both grass and cereal crops, although their long necks are better adapted for up-ending and reaching deeply submerged pond weeds. The nest contains up to eight pale green eggs.

imm.

**WHOOPER SWAN** *Cygnus cygnus* ▶
**Length** 60 (150 cm).
**Appearance** Adults white, with long, straight necks; beak wedge-shaped, lemon-yellow at base, black at the tip, lacking basal knob. Young birds pale grey.
**Distribution** Winter visitor to Britain and north-west Europe.

The walking stick-like carriage of the head and neck, and the yellow on the beak, help to separate whooper from mute swans (*C. olor*). Strangely, whooper swan wings are silent in flight, but the birds themselves often utter wild, bugle-like whooping cries, in contrast to the mute swan, which though not strictly mute, is restricted to quiet hisses and grunts. Whooper swans breed on the Arctic tundra, although occasionally a pair will remain in northern Scotland to breed. They are birds of remote freshwater lakes, marshes and flooded grazing land, quite often seen on sheltered coastal bays and brackish lochs in the north. Up to five pale yellow eggs are laid, in one clutch.

117

## BEWICK'S SWAN *Cygnus columbianus* ▶
**Length** 48 in (120 cm).
**Appearance** Adults detectably smaller than other swans, white-plumaged with a shorter, goose-like neck held straight and erect; beak goose-like, black with yellow patches at base. Young birds pale grey.
**Distribution** Winter visitor to Britain and north-west Europe.

Bewick's swans resemble small versions of whoopers (*C. cygnus*), although perhaps rather more goose-like in both size and in the ratio of neck to total body length. They have a musical, goose-like hooting call, and are vocal birds, travelling in family parties and maintaining a conversational chatter both in flight and when feeding on open grasslands. Bewick's swans are winter visitors from north-western Europe, travelling to western Europe from Arctic Russia, and many can be seen at reserves such as those owned by the Wildfowl Trust in Britain. Here, the naturalist Sir Peter Scott and his co-workers have found that their beak patterns are as individual as our fingerprints, making it possible to identify each bird, and allowing some fascinating studies of their social life. Three to five greenish-white eggs are laid in a single clutch.

## CANADA GOOSE *Branta canadensis* ▶
**Length** 30 in (75 cm).
**Appearance** Adults and young have black heads, necks and beak, with a white patch below the chin; body dark brown above, paler below; tail black with broad white bar.
**Distribution** Introduced to parts of Britain and northern Europe.

These are large geese, most often seen on flooded gravel pits and park lakes. Charles II was the first to introduce them from their native Canada, to embellish his ornamental waterfowl collections, and other European monarchs and nobles quickly followed suit. Subsequent imports saw the species widely kept in captivity, and frequent escapes from such collections have now established considerable feral populations in Britain and Scandinavia, many of which retain their tameness and tolerance of man. Year-round residents, rarely moving far, Canada geese can damage grassland by overgrazing. They are extremely territorial in the breeding season and may attack and often kill other waterfowl when living close to other birds. Up to six pale olive eggs are laid in one clutch.

**MALLARD** *Anas platyrhynchos* ▶
**Length** 23 in (58 cm).
**Appearance** Adult males have dark green head, rich brown breast, grey back, brown flanks and black-and-white upturned tail; legs orange; beak greenish yellow. Females, young and males (between July and September) speckled brown and black.
**Distribution** Resident throughout Britain and Europe.

The mallard is the 'wild duck' of old bird books, and remains the most widespread of ducks in Britain and Europe. The summer breeding population, living on remote marshes and lakes as well as farm ponds and park lakes, is joined in winter by migrants from the Continent, some of which remain on the coast in sheltered bays and estuaries. During courtship display, the male calls the female with an strange-sounding whistle, and the female signals her readiness to mate by coyly bobbing her head to one side. Sometimes the weight of the drake as he mounts her submerges the duck entirely as mating takes place. After mating, the drake swims in rapid circles round his female, before both bathe vigorously. Up to 12 greenish eggs are produced in a single clutch.

**TEAL** *Anas crecca* ▶
**Length** 14 in (35 cm).
**Appearance** A small duck; adult males have dark chestnut head with green mark through eye, brown back separated from grey flanks by black-and-white line; yellow patch in front of black undertail coverts. Females, young and eclipse males speckled grey-brown.
**Distribution** Resident throughout Britain and most of Europe; summer visitor to Scandinavia.

Among ducks only the garganey (*A. querquedula*) is as small and swift-flying as the teal, which tend to move about in groups, the males calling with a musical 'krit, krit . . .' Teal are very agile on the wing, dodging about like waders, and because they are such a difficult target, are popular quarry with wildfowlers. Compact groups can jump straight into flight off the water, which gives rise to the collective noun a 'spring' of teal. Teal are scarce breeding birds of wet grassland and bogs in central and southern Europe, although their numbers are augmented considerably in autumn and winter by migrants from further north. Teal are dabbling ducks, preferring thin slushy mud beside lakes, on marshes, or in estuaries, in which to feed. Usually up to 10 stone-buff eggs are laid in a single clutch.

**GARGANEY** *Anas querquedula* ▶
**Length** 15 in (38 cm).
**Appearance** Adult males have brown head, with bold white mark through eye; rest of body a variety of brown shades; forewings pale blue, conspicuous in flight. Females, young and eclipse males speckled pale grey-brown.
**Distribution** Summer visitor to most of Britain and Europe; winters in Spain.

Garganey are very scarce breeding birds in Britain and Europe, choosing reed-fringed marshland ditches or, more often, large wet or swampy areas with extensive reed-beds beside which to nest. Fast-flying and small, like the teal (*A. crecca*), they are best identified at a distance by the peculiar crackling call of the male (in the Middle Ages, when they were far more numerous, garganey were called 'Crackling Teale') and by the pale forewings clearly visible in both sexes in flight. Up to 11 creamy buff eggs are produced in a single clutch.

## WIGEON _Anas penelope_ ▶
**Length** 18 in (45 cm).
**Appearance** Drake wigeon is handsome, with chestnut head, gold crown, pink breast and finely marked grey flanks; in flight, a white oval patch is conspicuous on each wing. Ducks and juveniles are more uniformly clad in a mixture of distinctive warm cinnamon-brown feathers.
**Distribution** Winters in most of Britain and Europe; breeds in far north.

Most wigeon breed on the Arctic tundra: only a few pairs nest in western Europe, mostly in grass beside freshwater lochs and streams. Up to 10 creamy buff eggs are laid in a single clutch. Birds from the Arctic migrate south in autumn, many visiting our estuaries and freshwater marshes and remaining throughout the winter. They are dabbling ducks, up-ending in the shallows to find eel-grass (a marine angiosperm) and sea lettuce (an alga) or grazing on grass close to the water – an unusual food for ducks. In favoured areas flocks may be hundreds, or even thousands of birds strong, drawing attention to themselves by the piercing whistle which is uttered by the drakes. Numbers may be even higher in winters when severe weather causes their Continental resorts to freeze over.

## GADWALL _Anas strepera_ ▶
**Length** 20 in (50 cm).
**Appearance** Males greyish-brown with black undertail coverts. Females, young and eclipse males speckled brown. Both sexes have conspicuous black-and-white patch on trailing edge of wing and a chestnut patch in the midwing, visible in flight.
**Distribution** Breeds in Britain and northern Europe; winters in central, west and south-west Europe.

Although widespread across its British and European range, nowhere is the gadwall numerous.

The drake is by far the least colourful of the dabbling ducks, and its plumage – a mixture of shades of grey-brown, some of it finely vermiculated – has earned it the local name of 'grey duck'. Gadwall prefer quiet, reed-fringed lakes and pools or slow-moving streams with dense marginal vegetation, but will sometimes venture on to salt water. Up to 12 creamy buff eggs are laid in a single clutch.

**PINTAIL** *Anas acuta* ▶
**Length** 28 in (70 cm).
**Appearance** Adult males slim, with long neck and long pointed tail feathers; head and neck brown with white vertical mark; back and flanks grey. Females, young and eclipse males pale brown, boldly speckled with dark brown; short tailed.
**Distribution** Winters in most of Britain and Europe; breeds in far north.

Much of the length of the drake pintail is composed of tail feathers; these, and the long slim neck, give a very characteristic flight silhouette, and in some southern parts of Britain the old vernacular name of 'sea pheasant' is sometimes used. Although numerous in the north, pintails are one of the rarer breeding dabbling ducks in southern, central and western Europe, but in winter, numbers rise considerably and they are to be found on inshore coastal waters, particularly in sheltered estuaries, and beside larger fresh waters inland. When feeding in the shallows they will often up-end, using their long neck to reach water plants too deep for other ducks. Up to 12 greenish eggs are produced in a single clutch.

◀ **SHOVELER** *Spatula clypeata*
**Length** 20 in (50 cm).
**Appearance** Males have bottle-green head, brown back, white breast and chestnut flanks. Females, young and eclipse males speckled brown. Both sexes have massive, dark, spoon-shaped beak and pale blue-grey forewing conspicuous in flight.
**Distribution** Resident in much of Britain and Europe; breeds far north-east and winters far south-west.

Classic dabbling ducks, shovelers need shallow water with plenty of soft mud for feeding. This they scoop up, extracting small animals and seeds as it passes through whalebone-like filters at the edges of the massive beak. In the breeding season, shovelers will nest beside large lakes but seem to prefer reedy swamps and marshland dykes with plenty of cover. Usually up to 12 greenish-white eggs are laid in a single clutch. In the winter, they frequent a wider range of suitably shallow fresh, brackish or salt waters. On the water, the shoveler's head-down posture and massive beak are good distinguishing features, and this same heavy-headed appearance characterizes its flight.

**TUFTED DUCK** *Aythya fuligula* ▲
**Length** 17 in (43 cm).
**Appearance** Males have a black head with a purple sheen, drooping crest and golden eye; breast and back black; flanks and belly white. Females dark brown, paler beneath, often with small white patch at base of beak and a small crest. Young birds and eclipse males resemble females but lack crest.
**Distribution** Resident in north-west Europe (including Britain) and central Europe; elsewhere breeds in far north and winters in far south.

Tufted ducks may be found on many medium or large freshwater habitats. In the breeding season they prefer lakes and ballast pits with fringing reeds and preferably with islands offering safe nesting sites, and they will adapt readily, given reasonable nest seclusion, even to the lakes in town parks. Up to 12 greenish eggs are produced in a single brood. In winter, when numbers in the west and south are boosted by migrants from further north and east they can often be seen on reservoirs. They are only rarely found on even the most sheltered seas. Tufted ducks are neat divers, often jumping clear of the water as they submerge to search vegetation for the various aquatic animals on which they feed.

123

## POCHARD *Aythya ferina* ▶
**Length** 18 in (45 cm).
**Appearance** Males head chestnut, with black breast, and grey back and flanks. Females rufous-brown, paler on face and throat. Young resemble females; also eclipse males, but with greyer back.
**Distribution** Resident in central and north-west Europe (including Britain); elsewhere breeds in far north and winters in far south.

Like many of the diving ducks, pochard tend to drift out into the more open water when disturbed, rather than flying off. If they do need to fly, take-off is achieved after a long pattering run across the water; another feature typical of diving ducks. In contrast, most surface-feeding or dabbling ducks can spring straight from the water surface into flight. Rare breeding birds in western Europe, pochard favour secluded and extensively reed-fringed ditches and lakes, but in winter, when numbers are swelled by migrants, they can be seen upon a wide range of open freshwater habitats including reservoirs and occasionally estuaries. They dive quite deep for their food, which is predominantly the roots, buds, leaves and seeds of aquatic plants. Up to 11 greenish eggs are laid in a single clutch.

## GOOSANDER ▶
*Mergus merganser*
**Length** 25 in (63 cm).
**Appearance** Males have bottle-green head with drooping crest and black back; underparts white, tinged pink in summer. Females have grey body; head and drooping crest chestnut. Both sexes have slender red beak. Young birds and eclipse males resemble females.
**Distribution** Breeds in north-west Europe (including Britain); winters in west and central Europe.

The largest and most spectacular of the 'saw-billed' ducks – fish-eating specialists with serrated beaks. As with the mergansers, their streamlined cigar-shaped body is a distinctive feature on the water and in flight. Goosanders tend to nest further inland, and higher in the hills than mergansers, but choose the same clear rivers and streams. Such streams also harbour good stocks of trout, and conflict between the saw-billed ducks and anglers has resulted in both goosanders and mergansers being persecuted. Goosanders are cavity nesters, sometimes choosing a hole in the river bank but more commonly a hollow tree, often several feet above the ground. Up to 13 white eggs are laid in a single brood. Although they cannot fly when they leave the nest, the young seem to come to no harm when, at a day or so old, they jump to the ground.

◀ **MARSH HARRIER** *Circus aeruginosus*
**Length** 21 in (53 cm).
**Appearance** Adult males brown bodied; wings brown, grey and black; long, pale grey tail. Adult females rufous-brown, head cream with dark mark through eye. Young uniformly dark brown.
**Distribution** Widespread in Europe (with some

in Britain) during summer; restricted to southern Europe in winter.

Although marsh harriers are still numerous in some wetland areas of Europe, drainage and destruction of the extensive reed-bed areas which are their favoured habitat has reduced drastically the breeding population to just a few pairs in some areas. Passage migrants, and especially young birds, are more frequently seen over a variety of habitats. The nest, into which four or five dull white eggs are laid, is an untidy and substantial platform of reeds, situated deep in the reed-beds which provide a range of food from frogs to ducklings.

**OSPREY** *Pandion haliaetus* ▶
**Length** 23 in (58 cm).
**Appearance** Brown back, wings and tail; white head with dark mark through eye; white underparts with speckled band across breast; wings pale below, darker at tips and with dark patch at 'wrist'.
**Distribution** Breeds in extreme north and north-east Europe (including Scotland); winters in extreme south-west.

Exclusively fish-eaters, ospreys can be seen hovering clumsily over lakes and streams before plunging, with a considerable splash, to emerge clutching a fish torpedo-like in sharp talons. The sides of the feet resemble coarse emery paper, as an additional aid in grasping slippery prey. Ospreys are now making a successful comeback in Britain. Migrants may be seen in any part, but the breeding summer visitors are largely confined to the Scottish Highlands, building bulky nests of branches in loch side pines into which they lay two to three pale eggs, densely spotted with dark brown.

**CRANE** *Grus grus* ▶
**Length** 44 in (110 cm).
**Appearance** Tall and heron-like with long legs and neck; adult body grey, with very bulky-tailed appearance; neck black-and-white; small red patch on crown. Young birds dull pale grey.
**Distribution** Breeds in north and north-east Europe (excluding Britain); winters in the south-west.

Cranes fly with both neck and legs extended – a useful separation feature from the similar grey heron (*Ardea cinerea*), which carries its neck retracted. They are scarce and irregular visitors other than on their breeding grounds and ancestral migration routes, and are most likely to be seen passing high overhead on autumn migration, blown off-course by easterly winds as they move south from their tundra breeding grounds in northern Europe. The call often draws attention first: a deep, metallic, trumpeting whoop. There are usually two buff or olive eggs with dark brown spots.

## WATER RAIL *Rallus aquaticus* ▶
**Length** 11 in (28 cm).
**Appearance** Adult head and breast grey; back dark brown; flanks barred grey-and-white, under-tail coverts white; beak long, slender, red at base with darker tip. Young birds duskier, with more extensively barred underparts.
**Distribution** Resident throughout Britain and Europe.

Although widespread in Britain and Europe, water rails are rarely numerous in the dense swampy or reed-bed areas in which they live. They are among the shiest of birds, their long toes and slender bodies allowing them to slip easily between plants and remain out of sight. They are more often heard than seen and their calls, particularly during the breeding season when they frequently call at night, have been likened to the squealing of a pig about to be slaughtered. Resident British birds are joined by Continental immigrants during the winter, and it is during freezing weather that water rails are most likely to be seen, as they are forced into the open to hunt for food, which besides the usual worms and insects, occasionally includes unwary small birds. Up to 11 cream-coloured eggs, peppered with dark red, are laid in two clutches.

## SPOTTED CRAKE *Porzana porzana* ▶
**Length** 9 in (23 cm).
**Appearance** Adults with short, dark-tipped yellow beak and greenish legs and feet; streaked brown above, grey below with pale spots on the breast and pale bars on the flanks; under-tail feathers buff.
**Distribution** Widespread summer visitor; winters in south-west Europe.

Although very scarce birds in Britain and Ireland, almost every year a few pairs will breed in suitable densely vegetated marshland. They are very skulking summer migrants, and will sometimes over-winter. Spring is the only time they draw attention to themselves with a regularly repeated abrupt whip-lash call, and periods of song from the male may continue through much of the night. Eight to twelve olive-buff, brown-spotted eggs are laid.

## ◀ MOORHEN *Gallinula chloropus*
**Length** 13 in (33 cm).
**Appearance** Adults brownish black with white streak along flanks and white under-tail feathers; forehead fleshy; red beak with yellow tip; legs green. Young birds grey-brown, paler below.
**Distribution** Resident throughout Britain and Europe.

Very few freshwater areas, from slow-flowing rivers and large lakes with well-vegetated margins down to the humblest marshland ditch or farmland pond, are without moorhens. They have a wide-ranging diet, for although they mainly eat vegetable matter they will eat all sorts of small animals. They quickly adapt to a diet of bread in town parks and become very tame. The nest is often a conspicuous pile of dead reeds, on an islet or overhanging branch, and the moorhens often manage to rear three broods in the summer. Each clutch is from five to eleven eggs, which are buff with brown spots. In part this is achieved by the assistance given by the fully-grown young of the first brood in feeding later broods.

**COOT** _Fulica atra_ ▶
**Length** 15 in (38 cm).
**Appearance** Adults uniformly dull black, with white fleshy forehead and white beak; legs grey with conspicuously lobed toes. Young birds grey-brown, paler below.
**Distribution** Resident throughout Britain and Europe.

Coot are more gregarious than moorhens (_Gallinula chloropus_), which tend to move in family groups or pairs. Large flocks of coot, often hundreds strong, can accumulate during the winter months. Coot favour larger expanses of water than moorhens, and dive, often deeply, for their plant food, usually well away from the reeds. In the breeding season they are noisy and aggressive, rival males swimming towards each other, wings raised and heads lowered, uttering metallic clucks. Sometimes the birds will fight, both birds rearing up and kicking with their feet. This always results in much splashing and sometimes injury to a participant. Four to eight eggs are laid, which are stone-coloured freckled with brown.

**LITTLE RINGED PLOVER** _Charadrius dubius_ ▶
**Length** 6 in (15 cm).
**Appearance** Adults sandy-brown above, white below; conspicuous black-and-white head pattern, with yellow eye-ring visible at close range; black collar. Young browner than adults, lacking black collar; no wing-bar visible in flight.
**Distribution** Widespread summer visitor to Britain and Europe.

Smaller than the closely related ringed plover (_C. hiaticula_), little ringed plovers show a marked preference for inland freshwater breeding sites. More often than not these are man-made, and include major excavations for road works and reservoirs, and sand, ballast and chalk pits. Here the birds will sit tight, well camouflaged, despite giant earth-moving machinery rumbling close past them. Four eggs are laid, and these are grey-buff peppered with brown spots.

## JACK SNIPE *Lymnocryptes minimus* ▶
**Length** 8 in (20 cm).
**Appearance** Adults and young a richly patterned mixture of browns, buffs and chestnut above; beak moderate length; legs greenish.
**Distribution** Breeds in extreme north-east Europe; winters in west, central and southern Europe.

Much smaller than snipe (*Gallinago gallinago*), jack snipe are silent when flushed – usually not rising until danger is imminent and then flying only a short distance, low and straight, before diving back into cover. Most can be seen on fresh or brackish swampy areas with dense vegetation, where they probe for food much like their larger relatives. So heavily do they rely on their excellent camouflage that few are disturbed and seen, so the jack snipe may be more numerous and widespread than we suspect. Usually four dark olive eggs are laid, and these are marked with blackish spots.

## SNIPE *Gallinago gallinago* ▶
**Length** 11 in (28 cm).
**Appearance** Adults and young have streaky chestnut-buff and brown plumage on their backs and three bold yellowish stripes on the crown; beak very long, straight.
**Distribution** Resident in Britain, north and central Europe; elsewhere winters in west and south.

Snipe live in fresh or brackish marshland areas with plentiful soft mud for feeding, and with dense fringing vegetation in which they can take cover if danger threatens. When flushed, snipe fly off in a characteristic zig-zag flight pattern. The bones of the skull and beak are flexible and so arranged that they can slide over one another. This allows snipe to probe deep into the mud for worms, locating them by touch (the beak tip has many sensitive nerve endings), and then opening just the tips of the beak to seize and pull them free without taking a beakful of mud at the same time. Usually four grey-brown eggs with many brown spots are laid.

## ◀ GREEN SANDPIPER
*Tringa ochropus*
**Length** 9 in (23 cm).
**Appearance** Upperparts dark greyish with a few white flecks; underparts white with dark streaks on breast; rump white; tail with dark bars at tip; legs greenish.
**Distribution** Breeds in north and north-east Europe; winters in south and south-west Europe.

Primarily passage migrants, wintering in Africa as well as the Mediterranean and breeding in northern and central Europe, green sandpipers now winter regularly in small numbers on suitable marshland creeks in Britain and Ireland. They appear almost black with a striking white rump in flight, and have a musical yodelling call. Their breeding grounds are wooded swamps, and green sandpipers will occasionally use the deserted nests of birds such as thrushes, in trees well clear of the ground – a most unusual nest site for a wader. The nest usually contains four greenish-buff eggs, sparsely marked with dark brown spots.

## WOOD SANDPIPER _Tringa glareola_ ▶
**Length** 8 in (20 cm).
**Appearance** Upperparts dark grey-brown, with conspicuous white flecking in summer; crown dark; conspicuous pale eye-stripe, underparts mainly white, flecked with brown on throat; rump white, tail with many fine dark bars; legs yellowish.
**Distribution** Summer visitor to most of Europe; breeds in the north.

Smaller and more slimly built than the green sandpiper (_T. ochropus_), wood sandpipers choose much the same fresh or brackish marshland as their prime habitat. In flight they are lighter coloured than green sandpipers, and the barred tail reduces the conspicuousness of the rump. A further clue to their identity is the wood sandpiper's 'chiff-iff iff' call. Most wood sandpipers are seen in Britain on spring and autumn passage to and from their northern European breeding grounds, but a few pairs now breed in the Scottish Highlands, nesting either on the ground in swampy woodland or, less often, in the deserted nests of other birds in trees. The nest usually contains four greenish-buff eggs, boldly spotted purple-brown.

## COMMON SANDPIPER _Actitis hypoleucos_ ▶
**Length** 8 in (20 cm).
**Appearance** Upperparts brownish, with white flecks in summer; underparts white, with brown streaks on throat and breast; rump and centre of tail dark; legs greenish.
**Distribution** Widespread summer visitor; winters in western and southern Europe.

During the breeding season, common sandpipers are characteristic birds of sparkling clear, fast-flowing streams in upland areas. Usually four eggs are produced, yellowish white with many brown flecks. The common sandpipers' whirring flight on stiff, down-curved wings low over the water, their habit of bobbing incessantly when standing or walking, and their trilling call are all useful aids to identification. Elsewhere they are common passage migrants, visiting swampy areas ranging from natural fresh and salt marshes to man-made habitats such as gravel pits and sewage farms.

## REDSHANK *Tringa totanus* ▶
**Length** 11 in (28 cm).
**Appearance** Grey-brown above with darker streaking; pale below with heavy dark streaks; white belly and rump; plumage colour richer in summer; white wing-bar conspicuous in flight; legs bright red; brown in young birds.
**Distribution** Resident in many parts of Europe (including Britain); breeds in north, north-west and east; winters in west and south-west of Europe.

With the bold white trailing edge to the wing, redshanks are conspicuous on the damp grassland or moorland and fresh, brackish and salt marshes which form their home right across Britain and Ireland, throughout the year. Their shrill yelping cries and habit of hovering over the head of any intruder in their territory, shrieking loudly, have earned them colloquial names such as 'sentinel' or 'warden of the marshes': mostly from wildfowlers whose quarry they have alerted. Redshanks use their fine-tipped beaks to pick insects or other food items delicately off the surface of the mud or water or to probe deeply for buried worms or shellfish. They usually lay four eggs, buff with dark spots.

## TEMMINCK'S STINT ▼
*Calidris temminckii*
**Length** 5 in (13 cm).
**Appearance** A tiny wader; summer adults mottled buffish-brown above, white below with faint buff markings on breast; legs yellowish. Winter adults and young drab grey, shading gradually to white below.
**Distribution** Breeds in parts of northern Europe (including Britain); usually seen elsewhere as a passage migrant.

Generally much scarcer than the little stint (*C. minuta*), Temminck's stints have a more southerly breeding area in northern Europe and a few pairs have bred in remote Scottish moorland areas, laying up to four greenish-grey eggs spotted purple-brown. Most often seen on fresh or brackish wetlands, coastal or inland, it is winter plumage birds that are most familiar in Britain and Ireland. Their call – which sounds like a ruler scraped along railings – is distinct from the little stint's sharp 'chit', and in flight the outermost tail feathers are white, not grey.

## LITTLE STINT *Calidris minuta* ▶
**Length** 5 in (13 cm).
**Appearance**
A tiny wader; white below, chequered buff and brown above in summer, with an indistinct double 'V' marking on the back; legs black. Winter adults and young are uniform grey-brown above, still with 'V' marking.
**Distribution** Occurs over much of Britain and Europe as a passage migrant.

One of the smallest waders, little stints visit freshwater or brackish wetlands of all types, with exposed muddy areas in which they can probe for food with their short beak. They occur both on the coast and inland over much of Britain and Europe, and most are seen at migration times, although a few may remain through the winter in warmer areas in mild years. In flight, the 'V' pattern on the back is a useful feature, as are the smoky grey outer tail feathers, contrasting with the dark centre to the rump and tail. Three to four greenish-buff eggs with dark brown spots are laid in a single clutch.

## RUFF *Philomachus pugnax* ▶
**Length** Males 12 in (30 cm); females 9 in (23 cm).
**Appearance** Summer males show a wide variety of colours (white, chestnut, black) of the 'ruff' feathers, overlapping the breast and back, back mottled rich brown; underparts white. Smaller females mottled rich buffs and browns. Both sexes resemble drab female in winter.
**Distribution** Summer visitor to Britain and northern Europe.

Widespread and sometimes common in wetland areas across northern Europe, ruffs are now making a comeback in the western extremes of their range, where drainage had reduced numbers greatly. In spring, the males gather on a display arena (or lek) and erect their ruffs and indulge in posturing and sometimes in combat. The inconspicuous females wait nearby, select their mate, and after copulation build a nest and raise the family, usually nearby, on their own. They usually lay four greenish eggs with dark markings. In the much less distinctive winter plumage, the two white oval patches on the rump are useful identification features.

131

summer

winter

**BLACK TERN** *Chlidonias niger* ▶
**Length** 10 in (25 cm).
**Appearance** Breeding adults grey above, jet-black below with shallowly forked tail; wings dark grey above, almost white below. Winter adults grey above, white below, with black half-collar. Young birds similar but mottled with brown.
**Distribution** Breeds over much of Europe.

Black terns nest in colonies on inland fresh waters over much of Europe – laying up to four brownish eggs blotched with black – but only occasionally breed in Britain and Ireland. Most are seen here on spring migration (in breeding plumage) and in autumn, when they may be in any plumage or between plumage moult. Most occur on reservoirs or lakes, and feed typically by flying along slowly, a few feet above the water and suddenly dipping down to skim an insect from the surface.

◀ **SWIFT** *Apus apus*
**Length** 7 in (18 cm).
**Appearance** Adult sooty-black except for greyish throat; wings long, slender and sickle-shaped, tail shallowly forked. Young birds similar but with scaly grey markings on body.
**Distribution** Summer visitor to almost all of Britain and Europe.

Swifts are among the latest migrants to return from African winter quarters, and one of the earliest to leave, but throughout the summer 'screaming parties' are a common sight, flying at high speed through the streets of the older parts of towns and cities. Although the beak is apprently tiny, the swift's mouth opens almost from ear to ear; this huge gape is well suited to the bird's diet, which is entirely composed of insects caught on the wing. Among the most aerial of birds, swifts feed, sleep and even mate in flight. They may fly at great altitudes, and travel hundreds of kilometres in search of good weather and the consequent rich food supply. Swifts lay up to four dull white eggs in a single brood.

◄ **KINGFISHER** _Alcedo atthis_
**Length** / in (18 cm).
**Appearance** Unmistakeable; electric blue-green above, vivid chestnut below, with white throat and cheek patches; long, dagger-shaped dark beak, tiny scarlet feet.
**Distribution** Resident in most parts of Britain and Europe; summer visitor to extreme north.

Kingfishers are birds of placid, reed-fringed lakes or clear streams with plenty of overhanging vegetation for use as fishing perches, and with stretches of low, earthy banks in which they can excavate their nest burrows. The nest contains up to seven round, white eggs, and there are two broods. The nest is so slimy and smelly and full of fish scales that the adult emerging from the entrance often takes a bath in the stream before flying off to search for food.

**PIED/WHITE WAGTAIL** _Motacilla alba_ ►
**Length** 7 in (18 cm)
**Appearance** Nimble birds with long black legs and long, constantly flicking tail. Adults boldly pied but juveniles are browner with less distinct markings. Mantle of white wagtail pale grey; that of the pied black in male and grey in female.
**Distribution** Widespread British and European resident; summer visitor to north-east Europe.

These wagtails are well known for their opportunist use of man-modified habitats. Their characteristic 'chisick' flight call is a common sound throughout the whole of Europe and Asia, even in city centres. The nest of moss, leaves, roots, grass and twigs, lined with hair, wool or feathers is built by the hen and sited in holes in walls, sheds and banks or hidden among ivy or wood piles, etc. The nest contains five or six bluish or off-white eggs, speckled with grey. Relatively bare ground, such as roads, lawns or waste-ground, is preferred for feeding, the constant tail-wagging of the birds only ceasing during rapid dashes after insects. The white wagtail (_M. a. alba_) is the Continental race, chiefly a coastal passage migrant in the British Isles, and only breeding in Britain sporadically. Pale grey upperparts distinguish it from the pied wagtail (_M. a. yarrellii_).

### GREY WAGTAIL ▶
*Motacilla cinerea*
**Length** 7 in (18 cm).
**Appearance** Unmarked grey upperparts and bright yellow underparts; yellow undertail coverts and very long, white-edged, black tail; in summer, male has small black bib and female has white bib; juveniles browner above and less yellow below.
**Distribution** Widespread British and European resident.

In all seasons and plumages the grey wagtail's bright yellow rump and undertail coverts, grey back and very long tail make identification easy in their fast-flowing river haunts in Britain and Europe. Their call – a high-pitched, metallic 'tzitzi' – is also distinctive. In their search for insects, crustaceans and tiny molluscs, grey wagtails show remarkable agility, plucking prey from the water's edge and flitting from rock to rock in mid-stream. Well-hidden river bank crevices provide natural nest sites, but holes in bridges, weirs and buildings are also used.

As a resident species, dependent upon running water for feeding sites, and breeding at high altitudes in mountainous regions, grey wagtails suffer badly during hard winters, but populations usually recover quickly. The nest contains between four and six cream-coloured eggs, densely speckled with greys and browns.

### YELLOW WAGTAIL *Motacilla flava* ▲
**Length** 7 in (18 cm).
**Appearance** Males typically have bright yellow head and underparts, and olive-green back. males in autumn plumage and females and young birds are duller: browner above and paler yellow below, the young with dark, necklace-like markings.
**Distribution** Widespread summer visitor to Britain and Europe.

Throughout their breeding range, males of this species show a marked geographical variation in head patterning and colour, at least 13 races having been described. In Continental western Europe, the British yellow-headed race is replaced by the blue-headed wagtail, some of which occur and even breed in Britain each year. Male yellow wagtails arrive at their breeding sites and establish territories some two weeks before the females arrive, and five or six greyish-white eggs, closely spotted with brown, are laid in one or two broods. Coastal marshes and inland water meadows are their preferred habitats, although some nest in market garden areas, and most frequent drier habitats while migrating to and from their winter quarters in tropical West Africa. Leaving their communal reed-bed roosts at dusk, yellow wagtails complete this 3000 mile (4828 km) journey in about 30 days, averaging 100 miles (160 km), or four hours' flying, each day.

**DIPPER** *Cinclus cinclus* ▶
**Length** 7 in (18 cm).
**Appearance** Upperparts dark chestnut brown; tail brown, often cocked; throat and upper breast white, with chestnut border merging into the black belly. Young birds dark grey above, paler below, with plentiful white markings.
**Distribution** Widespread resident throughout Britain and Europe.

Dippers are birds of sparkling streams flowing over pebbly rapids, with a plentiful supply of large boulders as perches. In Britain and Ireland they are most numerous, year-round, in the west and north. Dippers have a unique feeding technique: after bobbing up and down on a mid-stream boulder, they slip off into the passing torrent, some wading waist-deep in the shallows, others submerging completely. Beneath the surface they seek small freshwater animals, and in deep water they may swim, sheathed in a silver air-bubble, using their wings for propulsion. After bobbing to the surface, they may whirr away, low over the water, to another stretch of the river territory. Dippers usually lay four to six glossy white eggs, and there are two broods.

**CETTI'S WARBLER** *Cettia cetti* ▶
**Length** 6 in (15 cm).
**Appearance** Rich reddish-brown above, with a long, rounded tail; white eye-stripe; underparts whitish, shading to buff on the flanks.
**Distribution** Resident in south, south-west and western Europe (including Britain).

The range of Cetti's warbler in Europe has been expanding steadily in recent decades. Unlike most warblers they are residents and are therefore vulnerable to food shortage in the winter, but since colonizing south-east England in the early 1960s, their breeding numbers have steadily increased despite several hard winters. They lay usually four red-brown eggs and there are two or more broods. Cetti's warblers are secretive birds, difficult to see well in their preferred habitat, which is usually dense vegetation fairly close to marshland. Their presence is best detected by their song – an explosive burst from deep in a bush, sounding like 'chee, chee-*wee*-choo'.

### GRASSHOPPER WARBLER ▶
*Locustella naevia*
**Length** 5 in (13 cm).
**Appearance** Upperparts streaked with dark brown, sometimes reddish-brown; underparts whitish or buffish, with faint darker streaks on breast.
**Distribution** A widespread summer visitor to Europe (including Britain), except for the south-west.

Although widespread over much of Britain (except Highland Scotland) and Ireland, grasshopper warblers are nowhere common. They are extremely secretive birds of marshland or dense damp vegetation bordering marshes, but occasionally colonize young conifer plantations and other densely vegetated but relatively dry areas. Although it is difficult to get a glimpse of these birds, they often give away their presence by their song. Often produced in the evening, or at night, the song is a sustained, high-pitched trilling, reminiscent of the clicking ratchet on a reel as fishing line is run out. Up to six pinkish eggs, densely freckled with red-brown are laid; one brood in the north of their range, two in the south.

### SAVI'S WARBLER *Locustella luscinioides* ▲
**Length** 6 in (15 cm).
**Appearance** Olive-brown above, with relatively long wedge-shaped tail; buff below; paler, almost white, on throat and belly.

**Distribution** Summer visitor to much of Europe (including Britain).

Savi's warblers are widely distributed throughout central Europe (less so in the Iberian Peninsula) but are nowhere numerous. Forced into extinction in Britain over a century ago by marshland drainage, they staged a recolonization comeback in the 1950s. Their song is very similar to that of the heavily streaked grasshopper warbler – whose call resembles a fishing reel running out. Savi's warblers sing in shorter bursts and with a deeper tone. Savi's warblers lay up to six whitish eggs, densely spotted with grey-brown, and there are two broods.

## GREAT REED WARBLER ▶
*Acrocephalus arundinaceus*
**Length** 8 in (20 cm).
**Appearance** Upperparts greyish olive-brown, slightly reddish on the head with a pale eye-stripe; underparts whitish, washed with warm buff on the breast.
**Distribution** Widespread summer visitor to Europe, except for the north.

These massive, thrush-sized warblers are widespread but rarely numerous in damp vegetation in marshes, along rivers and around lakes over much of Europe. Summer visitors from Africa, in Britain they remain only rare – although annual – visitors, occurring during the summer or autumn. Should they choose to settle, their strident, even raucous, song, produced from a perch high on a reed, quickly alerts birdwatchers to their presence. The nest contains up to six pale blue eggs, boldly spotted dark brown.

## REED WARBLER *Acrocephalus scirpaceus* ▶
**Length** 5 in (13 cm).
**Appearance** Reddish-brown above, with relatively long wedge-shaped tail; faint white eye-stripe; whitish below, shading to buff on flanks and breast.
**Distribution** Widespread summer visitor to Europe (including Britain), except for the north.

As their name implies, reed warblers are birds of reed-beds and other dense aquatic vegetation. They build a nest skilfully woven on to several reed stems, into which they lay up to five greenish eggs, flecked with brown. This is sufficiently strong to support even the weight of a well-grown cuckoo chick, for reed warblers are the commonest cuckoo 'foster parents' in wetland habitats. Studies of ringed reed warblers show that they put on little weight prior to the autumn southward migration which is undertaken in easy stages – in contrast to that of the sedge warbler (*A. schoenobaenus*).

**MARSH WARBLER** *Acrocephalus palustris* ▲
**Length** 5 in (13 cm).
**Appearance** Greenish or yellowish olive-brown above; buff, sometimes yellow-tinged below; legs pinkish.

**Distribution** Summer visitor to central, northern and eastern Europe.

Despite having similar plumage, song and habitat choice quickly separate reed (*A. scirpaceus*) and marsh warblers from each other. The song of the marsh warbler, though similar in structure to that of the reed warbler, is much richer and full of mimicry, particularly mimicking birds with tinkling songs like the goldfinch. Marsh warblers live and nest in damp shrubby areas such as nettles, willowherb and meadowsweet rather than reed-beds. The nest is woven between stout vertical stems, and typically has securing 'basket handles' at each point of attachment. Up to five bluish eggs with a few heavy dark blotches are laid.

## SEDGE WARBLER▶
*Acrocephalus schoenobaenus*
**Length** 5 in (13 cm).
**Appearance** Upperparts brown, with darker streaks; dark-edged white eye-stripe; underparts buff, paler on throat.
**Distribution** Widespread summer visitor to Europe (including Britain), except for the south-west.

Sedge warblers occur in wetland habitats, and nest, often away from the water, low down in dense vegetation. Up to six pale eggs are laid, densely speckled with brown, and there are often two broods. Although repetitive, their song is more varied than that of the reed warbler (*A. scirpaceus*). Towards the end of the summer, sedge warblers feed actively on both insects and berries, quickly putting on fat to the extent that their weight may double. This fat is used as 'fuel', and burnt up on the long journey south. Ringing recoveries support the theory that many sedge warblers fly direct from Britain to Africa non-stop – a stupendous journey!

## FAN-TAILED WARBLER▶
*Cisticola juncidis*
**Length** 4in (10 cm).
**Appearance** Tiny; buff, heavily marked brown above, pale fawn below; rounded brown tail.
**Distribution** Resident in south and south-west Europe.

Fan-tailed warblers are a Mediterranean species and, unusually for warblers, are resident. They are birds of open, long-grass country and sedgy marshes, and are secretive and inconspicuous except when they burst briefly skywards uttering their plaintive 'zeek' song. Fan-tailed warblers have spread north through France in recent years, and the occasional British or Irish record may soon be joined by others if this increase in breeding range continues. Up to six buff eggs, finely spotted brown, are laid and there are two clutches.

## BLUETHROAT▶
*Luscinia svecica*
**Length** 6 in (15 cm).
**Appearance** Adult males in summer brown above with reddish edges to the tail; the throat is bright blue, fringed black and chestnut with a central white or chestnut spot. Females and winter males have whitish throat with dark speckled margins.
**Distribution** Summer visitor to north and north-east Europe.

These tuneful and extremely colourful songsters breed in the boggy tundra scrub of their northern breeding grounds. Bluethroats are annual visitors as migrants to Britain and Ireland – some in spring (when their beautiful plumage may be glimpsed) but more often in autumn. They are secretive birds, and often all that is seen is the characteristic chestnut-red and brown tail pattern as a dark, robin-like bird darts into the depths of a bush. The nest contains up to seven greenish eggs with red-brown spots.

## ◀ BEARDED TIT *Panurus biarmicus*
**Length** 6 in (15 cm).
**Appearance** Adult males have dove-grey crown, chestnut back and long tail; broad black moustachial stripes; underparts white, buff on flanks, black beneath tail. Females and young long-tailed; tawny brown above, paler below.
**Distribution** Rather patchily distributed resident of Britain and Europe.

Although acrobatic and appearing to 'do the splits' as they grasp the swaying stems of the reeds, bearded tits, or reedlings, are feeble in flight, whirring along on short rounded wings. Their prime habitat is extensive reed-beds, where they feed on the seeds of the reed *Phragmites*, and where the population suffers severely in winters of prolonged low temperatures or snowfall which flattens the reeds. Such is their breeding capacity, however, that given a good summer, each surviving pair may lay three (or even more) clutches of six or seven white eggs with grey-brown markings, and the reed-beds are soon resounding again to the distinctive 'ping-ping' calls of the fledgling young.

**PENDULINE TIT** *Remiz pendulinus* ▶
**Length** 4in (10 cm).
**Appearance** Adults brown backed and grey
hooded; black 'masks' over the eyes; underparts
fawn. Young birds browner.
**Distribution** Patchily distributed across
southern Europe.

Penduline tits, with their wheezy call, are birds of
willow-fringed wetlands in southern and south-
eastern Europe, building a retort-flask-shaped nest
of fluffy vegetable fibres. Even in their breeding
range their occurrence is sporadic, and penduline
tits are very rare stragglers to Britain.

**REED BUNTING** *Emberiza schoeniclus* ▶
**Length** 6 in (15 cm).
**Appearance** Summer males have bold black
head and throat; white breast and collar; brown
and chestnut-streaked back; tail dark with white
outer feathers. Females, young and winter males
browner; throat pale; head with dark chestnut
and brown markings.
**Distribution** Widespread British and European
resident; summer visitor only to north-east
Europe.

Widespread throughout the year in damp areas,
even at quite high altitudes, reed buntings, with
their rasping, monotonous four-note song, typify
wetland habitats. However, they are increasingly
spreading into farmland and young conifer plantations, even in relatively dry areas. The male
changes from his winter drabness to summer beauty
by the simple process of his feathers, dark glossy
black at the base but with buff or brown tips,
wearing out as winter progresses, revealing his full
plumage for display and at the same time reducing
the insulating properties of his feathers to suit the
oncoming summer. Four or five olive eggs are laid
with large dark spots; there are two broods.

# Coasts and estuaries

Europe's varied and extensive coastlines provide feeding and nesting opportunities for many bird species, from piratical skuas and great black-backed gulls, to dainty terns and colourful ducks. Throughout the year this is perhaps the richest habitat, with fresh supplies of food being made available with every turn of the tide.

The physical nature of the coastlines of Britain and Europe is extremely varied. Below the high water mark the seabed may be rocky, composed of shingle, sand or mud, or a mixture of sand and mud. The nature of the seabed is important to birdlife, because at low water it forms an important feeding ground. Shingle, for example, supports very few plants and small animals, since it is so mobile under wave action. It thus attracts few birds. Rocky seabeds allow seaweeds to develop, and a plentiful fauna of shellfish to flourish, and so mollusc-eating birds such as oystercatchers, turnstones and eiders are able to find rich pickings on rocky shores. Although the precise range of plants and animals inhabiting sand and mud may change with the type of seabed, they provide by far the richest feeding areas, often almost comparable in abundance and quality with an estuary.

The shoreline itself is also variable. On low-lying coasts, marshland may be protected by a man-made sea wall, or ranks of sand dunes thrown up by the sea itself may protect the hinterland. Apart from what their beaches have to offer, these shorelines rarely support large bird populations in winter or summer. (Dunes are an exception; those in areas remote from human disturbance may in summer hold huge gulleries or terneries.)

On rocky coasts, it is the nature of the rock (as well as the amount of fish in the adjacent seas) that tends to determine the seabird population. This is normally low in winter, when most seabirds are out at sea, but rises dramatically in favoured areas during the breeding season when the seabirds – most of which are colonial – come ashore to breed,

The pear-shaped egg of the guillemot is a masterpiece of evolutionary engineering, unlikely to roll off the nesting ledge if accidentally knocked.

forming veritable seabird cities. The cliffs and rock stacks need to be sufficiently precipitous to offer protection from land predators, and also need to be correctly angled to provide nest sites. If the rock is too crumbly – for example on chalk cliffs – then suitably strong ledges do not form, and breeding seabird numbers are low. Granites are tough and weather very slowly, and in some cases offer few ledges on which seabird colonies can form. Conversely, sedimentary rocks like limestone and sandstone do weather to form suitable ledges, but the strata must lie roughly horizontally for the ledges to be habitable.

Coastal areas can provide some of the most spectacular and exciting birdwatching, but it should be remembered that in these habitats it is the state of the tide that governs the lives of the birds. For instance, if feeding birds are sought, then the hours just before or just after high water are the best times to watch, as the sand or mud available for feeding is limited in extent and close inshore.

At or around high tide, those birds that feed by probing rather than by diving (mostly the waders and gulls) move to higher ground to roost, and here

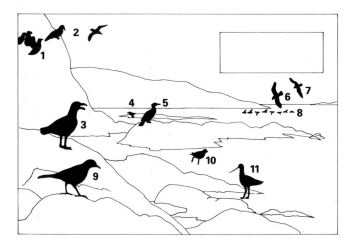

| | | | |
|---|---|---|---|
| 1 | guillemot (*Uria aalge*) | 7 | arctic skua |
| 2 | gannet (*Sula bassana*) | | (*Stercorarius pomarinus*) |
| 3 | herring gull (*Larus argentatus*) | 8 | common scoter |
| 4 | avocet | | (*Melanitta nigra*) |
| | (*Recurvirostra avosetta*) | 9 | rock pipit (*Anthus spinoletta*) |
| 5 | cormorant | 10 | grey plover |
| | (*Phalacrocorax carbo*) | | (*Charadrius squatarola*) |
| 6 | kittiwake (*Rissa tridactyla*) | 11 | black-tailed godwit |
| | | | (*Limosa limosa*) |

they can be observed at rest. The diving waders and the gulls are best seen on coasts and estuaries during autumn, winter and spring, but for the other seabirds such as auks, gannets and terns, the coast is at its most interesting during the summer months, when they all come ashore to nest.

Most seabirds gather in colonies for the breeding season. This is thought to offer them several collective advantages: the many pairs of eyes seeking rich feeding grounds are more likely to discover shoals of fish than a few birds hunting the seas alone, for example. Similarly, within the colony those many pairs of eyes will quickly detect an approaching predator, and the group response of mobbing the intruder may well either drive it away or at least distract it.

## BIRDS OF COASTS

The great majority of seabirds are birds of rocky, cliff-girt coastlines with deep, clear seas. The north and west coasts of Britain and Ireland abound in such areas, and place these islands among the best for seabirds in Europe, and indeed the world. The range of species is considerable, and the variety in their life-styles fascinating.

Perhaps best known are the gulls. These birds are versatile feeders, nowadays as common inland in winter as scavengers on refuse tips as they are on the coast. Most are found in coastal waters throughout the year, although the noisy kittiwake and the highly predatory great black-backed gull head for the open ocean in winter. Related to them are the terns, slimmer and lighter birds which merit their colloquial name 'sea swallows'. They are summer visitors, often feeding close inshore and diving to secure a small fish or shrimp, even off crowded holiday beaches. Also related are the

skuas, the pirates of the seabird world, which make part or most of their living by harassing other seabirds into dropping their food, which the skuas then eat.

The auks – puffin, guillemot, black guillemot and razorbill – are primarily marine birds, with a robust 'box-girder' skeleton well suited to protecting the vital organs during deep diving, and with short, stiff wings which are poor for flight but excellent for underwater propulsion. These are all fish feeders, but share the exploitation of the sea's bounty by choosing different fish or different feeding areas.

The most spectacular method of feeding of all the seabirds is shown by the gannet. This bird has a 6-ft (1.8-m) wingspan and plunge-dives from 50 ft (15 m) or more above the waves, to emerge triumphantly with a fish. Related to the gannet are the shag, a resident of clear waters off rocky coasts, and the cormorant, which occurs in all sorts of shallow seas.

Despite the threats posed this century by oil pollution, together with the massive egg collecting and trapping of adults that went on in the past to provide food for remote human island communities, many seabird populations are, happily, flourishing. One of the best examples of success is shown by the fulmar, which about 100 years ago was only found on St Kilda in the Outer Hebrides, but which now nests all round British and Irish coasts. Part of the fulmar's success lies in its feeding versatility and its ability to capitalize on offal thrown overboard by fishing boats, but as it only lays a single egg each year, the major reason must be its extraordinary length of life.

Mudflats are very rich in food, chiefly shellfish and worms living at various depths. To exploit these resources without excessive competition, estuarine birds exhibit a range of beak shapes and sizes.

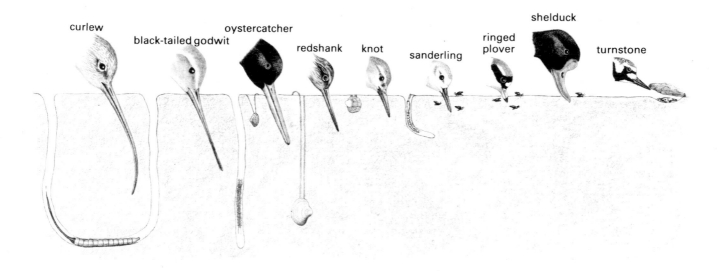

curlew    black-tailed godwit    oystercatcher    redshank    knot    sanderling    ringed plover    shelduck    turnstone

# BIRDS OF ESTUARIES

Estuaries are sheltered shallow inlets where sea meets river at the turn of the tide. Although it is the degree of shelter that most distinguishes the estuary from the open coast, the estuary layout – often as complex as a river delta – holds shallow waters which are both warm and rich in mineral and organic nutrients. This richness stems both from the sea and from the land water brought down by the river. Nestling in this warmth and shelter, and supplied with a rich abundance of food, most estuaries manage to develop copious wild life. Much of this is minute plant life in the form of algae, but it is also composed of millions of small animals like worms, molluscs and crustaceans.

An estuary has much the same superficial appearance all the year round. The mudflats themselves remain grey-brown, and the saltings islands, laced with runnels containing treacle-black mud, seem grey even in summer. The leaves of the tough grasses and the ubiquitous pinkish grey of the velvet-surfaced sea purslane help to impart this sombreness to the scene, although during the summer more colours appear as sea asters, sea lavender and golden samphire come into flower. In autumn the drier mudflats are given typical colours by the fleshy-stemmed glasswort.

Regular exposure and inundation as the tides ebb and flow are a feature of life for estuary vegetation, which in consequence must be tolerant of a wide range of salinities. Nevertheless, the algae and other microscopic plants feed many of the countless small animals; and larger plants, like sea lettuce (an alga) and eel-grass, are major food sources for typical estuary wildfowl like wigeon and Brent geese. Another typical mudflat plant is the rice-grass (*Spartina*); this plant is ecologically important, since silt accumulates between its robust stems, forming the foundations of the islands of the future. Masses of small snails seek shelter among clumps of *Spartina*, and these are noisily eaten by shelduck, which have a particular relish for them.

If any indication was needed, then the tremendous range of food supplies available is reflected in the feeding adaptations of the estuary birds as much as in their sheer numbers. On drier, sandier beaches at around the high tide mark, ringed plovers scamper about, picking up insects and other food with their stubby beaks. Further out on the mud or sand flats, other small, short-beaked waders probe for animal food just beneath the surface. The sanderling, ever active, its legs a blur as it dashes after a retreating wave to snatch up a delicacy it has revealed, is one of the smallest. The grey plover, bulky, silver-speckled and with conspicuous black 'arm-pits' in flight, is among the largest. Besides the waders, ducks – shoveler and teal paramount among them – sift through the mud for food. The shoveler, with its broad, spatulate beak and comb-like margins adapted to filter out food, is one of the most highly adapted of the ducks. It often squats belly-deep, contentedly feeding in the soft, liquid mud that it prefers.

The two most numerous estuarine birds are dunlin and knot. They often occur in flocks thousands strong – sometimes tens or even hundreds of thousands strong. As they fly, dunlin and knot twist and turn, one minute appearing grey, the next white, but in flocks so large that in the distance they look like wisps of smoke. How they avoid mid-air collisions is not really understood, but it is assumed that acute vision and split-second reflexes play a major part. Two of the noisiest estuary birds are the redshank – always on the alert and warning all and sundry of the approach of predator, wildfowler or birdwatcher alike – and the oystercatcher. The oystercatcher, at odds with man in some areas as it, too, eats cockles, is a skilful feeder. Its beak must be solid enough to knock limpets from their hold and at the same time delicate enough to insert, scissor-like, between the halves of a bivalve shell to snip the powerful muscle that clamps them shut.

The deepest-living worms and shellfish are pursued by the long-billed waders: the black and bar-tailed godwits and the curlew; each is capable of probing more than 4 in (10 cm) into the ooze.

The use of estuaries by birds is strongly seasonal. Although the feeding they offer is expansive and rich, good nest sites are few in number, and breeding birds are often limited to a few waders like redshank and the occasional colony of black-headed gulls or common terns. In some ways this seasonality enhances their importance, because many estuaries serve as staging posts; centres where wader populations can rest, perhaps moult, and certainly feed up for the next stage of their journey south to African winter quarters in autumn, or north to Arctic tundra breeding grounds in spring.

Thus the threats to our estuaries, mostly in terms of pollution or from industrial or port development on reclaimed ex-estuary land, should not be underestimated as their ecological importance is international in scale, leaving aside the pleasures and interests that they offer to the birdwatcher.

winter

## RED-THROATED DIVER *Gavia stellata* ▶
**Length** 22 in (55 cm).
**Appearance** Adults in summer white below, grey-brown above; head grey-brown; neck white, streaked brown, with dark red throat patch; beak slender, upturned, and often held pointing slightly upwards. In winter body white below, greyish-brown above, boldly flecked with white. Young resemble winter adults.
**Distribution** Resident in parts of northern Scotland and Scandinavia; winter visitor to Atlantic coasts and suitable habitats in central and western Europe.

Even quite tiny lakes over much of extreme northern Europe, sometimes well inland, may carry a pair of breeding red-throated divers. Some will breed beside sea lochs, and most will fly out to coastal waters to fish, often using their quacking or barking call as they go, later flying back inland with food for the young. Usually two, occasionally three dark-olive, elongated eggs are laid in a single clutch. Red-throated divers are appreciably smaller than black-throated (*G. arctica*) and great northern divers (*G. immer*), and in flight look paler and slimmer, with deeper, more frequent wing-beats. In winter, red-throated divers are mostly to be seen close inshore off the coast. They are more numerous in the south and occasionally venture on to inland fresh waters.

## MANX SHEARWATER ▼
*Puffinus puffinus*
**Length** 14 in (35 cm).
**Appearance** Adults upperparts completely blackish, underparts white. Young birds similar. The western Mediterranean race *mauretanicus*, is occasionally seen in British waters and is browner above with dusky underparts.
**Distribution** Summer visitor to Britain and western European coasts and Mediterranean islands; winters in Atlantic and Mediterranean.

Shearwaters are named after their characteristic flight pattern. Keeping close above the waves, they flap irregularly, often gliding on narrow wings held at right angles to the body. Usually one wing-tip is held low, 'shearing' the water, so that at each of the many changes of direction, birds show first white, then black. In winter, most migrate to South Atlantic waters, usually off Brazil, but a ringed bird has even reached Australia. In summer they breed, often in huge colonies, in underground burrows on remote headlands or uninhabited islands off rocky western coasts. Only one egg is laid, which is oval and white. They come ashore after dark to escape predation by gulls, and their eerie screeching cries are said to have given rise, in Scandinavia, to the legends of the trolls.

**FULMAR** *Fulmarus glacialis* ▶
**Length** 18 in (45 cm).
**Appearance** Adults superficially gull-like, but distinguished by tubular nostrils on the beak; body grey to grey-brown above, white below; wings grey, lacking black tips. Young resemble adults.
**Distribution** Summer visitor to British, Irish and Scandinavian coasts; winters in north Atlantic.

Fulmars are master gliders, making full use of the air currents over the waves to minimize energy use. So effective is their glide – first they turn and climb into the wind and then they glide down across the wind – that on a breezy day they may not flap their relatively short, stiff wings (usually held slightly down-curved from the dumpy body) for several minutes. Fulmars are successful birds: a century ago they were known in Britain only on the remote island of St Kilda, off the Outer Hebrides; now they breed round the entire British and Irish coastline, where they can be seen in most months of the year. A single, large whitish egg is laid, which is not replaced if lost. Part of the reason for their success may lie in their lifespan: the results of ringing studies suggest they may live for 30 years or more.

◀ **GANNET** *Sula bassana*
**Length** 36 in (90 cm).
**Appearance** Adults with cigar-shaped body and long slender wings; plumage white, with black wing-tips and yellow tinge to head in breeding season. Juveniles completely grey-brown in first year, gradually acquiring adult plumage over the next three years.
**Distribution** Summer visitor to the coasts of Britain and Europe; winters in the Atlantic and Mediterranean.

There can be few more spectacular sights than a flock of gannets plunging into the sea for fish. They dive from heights of 100 ft (30 m) or more, the birds letting their wings trail behind them in the split-second before they enter the water with a splash. Under water, they swim in pursuit of their prey – large fish – and, having caught one, bob up to the surface, swallowing it with a convulsive gulp. After a long run pattering across the surface, they take off to try again. Gannets breed in often large colonies, scattered round our rocky coasts. A single chalky blue egg is produced. Feeding some distance from home, they may in summer visit inshore waters.

## CORMORANT ▶
*Phalacrocorax carbo*
**Length** 36 in (90 cm).
**Appearance** Adults entirely blackish in winter, but with white patches on the face and thighs during the breeding season. Juveniles dark brown above, paler on throat and belly.
**Distribution** Resident on west coasts of Britain and Europe, and the Mediterranean.

Cormorants are occasionally found on large inland waters which are well stocked with fish where they sometimes breed. They are most often to be seen throughout the year in shallow coastal waters and estuaries, however. Like shags (*P. aristotelis*), they must occasionally dry their plumage to prevent waterlogging, and stand on buoys, piers, and navigation beacons, wings outstretched to dry in heraldic posture. They swim low in the water, diving from the surface and submerging with hardly a ripple. As shallow water feeders, they often catch flatfish and bring these to the surface to swallow them – often with some difficulty. Cormorants breed colonially, usually on low rocky islets or grassy cliffs, and in trees in freshwater habitats. Up to six chalky, pale blue eggs are produced; occasionally two broods.

**SHAG** *Phalacrocorax aristotelis* ▶
**Length** 30 in (75 cm).
**Appearance** Adults have completely dark plumage with an iridescent green sheen and no white patches; a curled-over head crest, conspicuous in spring, wears away by early summer. Juveniles are dark brown, uniform above and below.
**Distribution** Resident on west coasts of Britain and Europe, and Mediterranean.

Although difficult to distinguish at a distance, shags are slimmer, more lightly built and more agile than cormorants. Unlike cormorants (*P. carbo*), they are essentially maritime; only rarely are birds driven inland by storms. They favour the precipitous rocky coasts of western and northern Britain and Europe throughout the year, fishing at considerably greater depths and in clearer seas than cormorants. Shags breed on exposed ledges and in cavities beneath boulder tumbles, laying up to six small, chalky blue eggs. Young shags are strikingly reptilian in appearance, and as they grow are among the noisiest and smelliest of seabird young.

## GREYLAG GOOSE▶
*Anser anser*
**Length** 32 in (80 cm).
**Appearance** Adults upperparts dark grey, underparts paler; beak large, orange (western European race) or pink (eastern European race); legs pink. Young similar. Pale grey forewing conspicuous in flight.
**Distribution** Resident in north-west Scotland and north and north-west Europe; winter visitor to west and south-west Europe.

Greylags are the largest of our native wild geese and the ancestors, it is thought, of bulky farmyard geese. Their nasal gabbling calls – reminiscent, too, of the farmyard bird – are one of the best identification points, especially as in flight at a distance all the 'grey' geese look rather similar. A small population of greylags breeds in Britain – mostly in the Outer Hebrides – on heather moorland close to lochs, loch-islands and offshore islands. Until recently, most birds seen elsewhere were winter visitors to coastal marshes and stubble and harvested potato fields in the north, but now wildfowling clubs have established feral breeding populations in many parts of the country – both coastal and inland – so that the genuine 'wildness' of birds seen in winter must always be questioned. Greylags lay up to six creamy-white eggs, in a single clutch.

imm.

## WHITE-FRONTED GOOSE *Anser albifrons* ▶
**Length** 28 in (70 cm).
**Appearance** Adults dark grey-brown, darker on neck and head; white patch at base of pink (eastern race) or yellow (western race) beak; white beneath tail; heavy black barring on belly. Young birds lack the barring and the white face.
**Distribution** Winter visitor to Britain and north-west Europe.

Probably the commonest and most widespread of the grey geese visiting Britain and Ireland during the winter, white-fronted geese are birds of open pasture. They are often found on the rough grazing afforded by remote expanses of low-lying coastal

freshwater marshes, but white-fronts are occasionally seen inland and on arable fields, particularly those sown with winter wheat. They are one of the noisiest geese, with a high-pitched gabbling, yapping cry. Yellow-beaked birds seen in Ireland and western Scotland breed in Greenland, but the majority of British birds breed on the tundra of Arctic Russia. White-fronted geese lay up to six pale yellowish eggs, in a single clutch.

## ◀ BEAN GOOSE *Anser fabalis*
**Length** 30 in (75 cm).
**Appearance** Adults and young dark grey-brown, white beneath tail; lack pale forewing; legs yellow; beak yellow with a variable amount of black at base.

**Distribution** Winter visitor to Britain, north-west and central Europe.

Bean geese are an Arctic breeding species, nesting both on open tundra and in the broken forest at the edge of the tree line. The nest contains up to six yellowish eggs. They winter in a broad band from Italy and Greece north-west to Denmark and to Britain, where they are normally scarce visitors to some eastern counties. Throughout their winter range they prefer marshes and grazing fields, usually close to large rivers or lakes, rarely venturing on to arable farmland. Although less vocal than most geese, their low-pitched 'ung-unk' is a useful aid to identification at a distance.

## PINK-FOOTED GOOSE ▶
*Anser brachyrhynchus*
**Length** 26 in (65 cm).
**Appearance** Adults and young blue-grey above, brown below except for white beneath tail; head and neck noticeably dark; beak small, pink, black at base; legs and feet pink.
**Distribution** Summer visitor to Iceland; winter visitor to Britain and north-west Europe.

Of the wild grey geese, pink-footed geese are the lightest in build, and the grey back and forewings contrast sharply with the dark neck in flight. They produce a two- or three-syllable high-pitched 'wink-wink-wink' call. Pink-footed geese breed on the tundra, nesting on the ledges of rocky outcrops and river gorges in Greenland, Iceland and Spitzbergen, and laying up to five whitish eggs. As a wintering bird they are most numerous in Scotland, but a few are seen regularly in counties bordering the North Sea. Although sometimes found on rough grazing, pink footed geese show a preference for arable fields, feeding upon the post-harvest leftover cereals, carrots and potatoes.

dark-breasted        light-breas

## BRENT GOOSE *Branta bernicla* ▶
**Length** 24 in (60 cm).
**Appearance** Adults have black head and neck with white 'collar'; back dark grey, breast pale grey (western race) of dark grey (eastern race); white beneath tail. Young birds lack the white collar and have pale crescent-shaped marks on the back.
**Distribution** Winter visitor to Britain and western Europe.

Brent geese are very much birds of the sand and mudflats of sheltered coastal bays and estuaries. They are winter visitors from breeding grounds deep inside the Arctic Circle. Their prime food is the eel-grass *Zostera*, and when, 40 years ago, *Zostera* stocks were almost destroyed by disease, Brent goose numbers fell dramatically. Recently, the *Zostera* has recovered, and Brent goose numbers have risen rapidly, to the extent that when the *Zostera* has been too heavily grazed, the Brent geese turn their attention to the wheat crops planted on recently drained land just behind the sea walls, causing them to become pests to farmers. Brent geese lay up to five pale olive eggs, in a single clutch.

151

◄ **SCAUP** *Aythya marila*
**Length** 18 in (45 cm).
**Appearance** Males head black with green sheen; breast black, back grey; flanks white (all duller during eclipse). Females rich chestnut-brown, paler below, with large white face patch around base of beak. Young birds resemble females.
**Distribution** Winter visitor to coasts of Britain, north-west Europe and Mediterranean; breeds in far north of Europe.

Most scaup breed in the extreme north of Europe, the furthest south being the few pairs in Scotland nesting beside remote lochs. They are perhaps the most maritime of the diving ducks during winter. Scaup frequent sheltered bays and estuaries, sometimes in rafts (groups) thousands strong in the north as migrants from further north pass through or stay for the winter months. In the south numbers are generally much smaller although large, deep, freshwater habitats – usually close to the coast – are more frequently used. When feeding at sea, scaup are able to withstand rough weather, often straggling out in a long line as they dive through the breakers for their shellfish food. Up to 11 greenish eggs are laid in a single clutch.

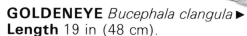

**GOLDENEYE** *Bucephala clangula* ▶
**Length** 19 in (48 cm).
**Appearance** Males have greenish-black head, with white patch on each cheek; black back, boldly marked with white; underparts white. Females body grey-brown; head chestnut. Young and eclipse males resemble females. All have large white patches on inner half of wing, striking in flight.
**Distribution** Breeds in far north and north-east Europe; winters in north-west and central Europe.

Goldeneyes are adept divers. During the winter months most are found in coastal localities, sometimes well out to sea, and they will continue diving for their fish, shellfish and crustacean food even in heavy seas. Some will overwinter on large, deep fresh waters such as reservoirs. Usually goldeneyes are found in small groups, characteristically close-knit and always diving, but off northern coasts much larger flocks can build up. Very scarce breeding birds in Britain, goldeneyes rather surprisingly choose cavities in trees beside Scottish Highland lochs in which to nest, and readily take to nestboxes set high on the trunk. Up to 12 bluish eggs are laid in a single clutch.

## COMMON SCOTER _Melanitta nigra_ ▶
**Length** 20 in (50 cm).
**Appearance** Males uniformly velvet black with black-and-yellow beak. Females dull dark brown, paler on sides of head. Young birds resemble females.
**Distribution** Breeds in far north of Europe including Britain; winters on west European coasts.

Common scoters breed along the far northern coasts of Europe, penetrating (as breeding birds) as far south as Scotland and Ireland. They nest on the shores of lakes and rivers, laying up to 12 creamy buff eggs in a single clutch. During the migration seasons and the winter months they are far more numerous and widespread, although most wintering birds are to be found around the coasts of southern and eastern Britain. Even far out to sea, long straggling lines of black and brown heavily built ducks, flying purposefully low over the waves are instantly identifiable as common scoter, the rarer velvet scoter (_M. fusca_) having a conspicuous white patch on the trailing edge of the wing. Common scoter are diving ducks, feeding mainly on shellfish.

## EIDER _Somateria mollissima_ ▶
**Length** 24 in (60 cm).
**Appearance** Males have black, white and green head, white back, black belly and pinkish breast. Females mottled dark brown. Young birds at first sight resemble females. Immature and eclipse males are blackish, showing a varying amount of white.
**Distribution** Resident in north-west Europe (including Britain) and Scandinavia.

The heavily built and strangely shaped head and beak of eiders – almost wedge-shaped in profile – hold powerful muscles that help the birds crush the shellfish which they obtain by diving in shallow coastal seas. Occurring off many parts of British, Irish and north European coasts in winter, breeding eiders are restricted to the north, most British representatives nesting in Scotland. On the nest, sitting females are exceptionally well camouflaged and tolerant of close human approach. Usually up to six greenish or buff eggs are laid in a single clutch. They pluck down from their breast to line the nest, and in Iceland this is systematically collected, almost on farming principles, to form an extremely efficient insulating filling for quilts and sleeping bags.

## SHELDUCK *Tadorna tadorna* ▶

**Length** 24 in (60 cm).

**Appearance** Head bottle green; neck and body white, with broad chestnut collar; black stripe on belly and much black visible on folded wing; legs pink, beak scarlet with conspicuous knob in male. Young grey and white.

**Distribution** Resident on coasts of north-west Europe (including Britain); winters in south and south-west Europe.

With their near goose-like appearance and pied plumage, shelducks are easy birds to identify. Most shelducks favour low-lying sandy or muddy coasts or estuaries which are well sheltered and suitable for their dabbling feeding, as they seek small shellfish in the ooze. The nest is often in a hollow, disused rabbit burrow or beneath dense vegetation, but occasionally pairs persist in nesting in old warrens some distance inland, leading their ducklings to the sea at a few days old, despite the hazards of crossing roads and railways. Up to 10 white eggs are laid in a single brood.

## RED-BREASTED MERGANSER ▼

*Mergus serrator*

**Length** 22 in (55 cm).

**Appearance** Males head and bristling crest green; throat white; breast chestnut; back black with grey-and-white flanks. Females pale brown, darker above, with pale chestnut crest. Both sexes have a slender reddish beak. Young birds and eclipse males resemble females.

**Distribution** Breeds in north-west Europe (including Britain); winters in west and central Europe.

Mergansers have characteristically streamlined silhouettes, and sit long and low in the water. When they dive, they make hardly a ripple, and once beneath the surface swim powerfully in pursuit of the fish that form the major part of their diet. The long beak is hooked at the tip and has serrated edges which help to grasp firmly their slippery prey. In the breeding season they nest in holes in the banks beside clear streams, and sometimes sea lochs. Up to 12 greenish or stone-coloured eggs are laid in a single brood. In the winter most mergansers head for coastal waters, chiefly in Scotland, but further south some are occasionally seen inland.

winter

**OYSTERCATCHER** *Haematopus ostralegus* ▶
**Length** 17 in (43 cm).
**Appearance** Adults have long orange beak and pink legs; upperparts black, underparts white; wings black with conspicuous white bar. Young birds duller, with scaly brown markings.
**Distribution** Resident in western Europe (including Britain) and the Mediterranean; this population is supplemented in winter by far-north breeding birds.

Oystercatchers, with their striking 'sea-pie' plumage and shrill, piping 'kleep' call, are a conspicuous feature of many coastal areas. In summer, some pairs nest well inland in moist river valley meadows in the north and west, when they lay two to four stone-coloured eggs flecked with black in a shallow scrape. Although it looks cumbersome, the beak can be used very skilfully as either scissors or chisel to open mussels or dislodge limpets from their hold on the rocks. Oystercatchers tend to specialize in their feeding habits, some taking worms, others limpets and others bivalves, including cockles. In some areas, this has led to conflict with humans because of alleged interference by the oystercatchers with the cockle fishing industry.

imm.

**RINGED PLOVER** *Charadrius hiaticula* ▶
**Length** 8 in (20 cm).
**Appearance** Adults sandy-brown above, white below; black-and-white facial pattern, broad black collar; short, yellow beak has black tip; conspicuous wing-bar in flight. Young browner, lacking collar.
**Distribution** Summer visitor to Britain and northern Europe, winters on the coasts of north-west, west and southern Europe.

Apart from their bold black collar, ringed plovers are well camouflaged as they run across the sandy beaches and estuaries where they feed and nest. The nest is little more than a scrape in the sand or shingle, and the eggs – usually four, buff-coloured with blackish spots – are among the masterpieces of bird camouflage, but all too easy to tread on accidentally. If a predator like a crow or fox approaches, ringed plovers will attempt to lure it away from the nest with the 'broken wing trick', feigning injury by trailing one wing and seeming to offer an easy target.

## KENTISH PLOVER ▶
*Charadrius alexandrinus*
**Length** 6 in (15 cm).
**Appearance** Adults pale sandy above, white below; chestnut crown; black on forehead and through eye, and black half-collar. Young birds browner, lacking black markings.
**Distribution** Resident of south and south-west European coasts.

The Kentish plover, neat-looking and fast-moving as it runs across sandy or stony flats close to the sea, is a predominantly Mediterranean bird in Europe, although breeding pairs occur up the Atlantic coast of France and the Low Countries. One of the most cosmopolitan of all waders, with a world-wide distribution and several different national names, it is now a rare visitor to the extreme west, occurring only as a migrant in Britain.

## GREENSHANK ▼
*Tringa nebularia*
**Length** 12 in (30 cm).
**Appearance** Pale grey-brown above; adults richly flecked with black in summer; white below with brownish spots on throat and breast; beak and legs green.

**Distribution** Breeds in northern Europe (including parts of Britain); winters in south-west and west.

Most greenshanks breed in the west tundra of northern Europe, although small numbers breed each year as far south as northern Scotland. Elsewhere in Europe, greenshanks are passage migrants, visiting wetlands both inland and on the coast. On a few sheltered estuaries in the milder west, especially in Ireland, greenshanks now overwinter regularly. Paler than either of the redshanks, and at least as large as the spotted redshank (*T. erythropus*), greenshanks have a triple-barrelled distinctive 'tu-tu-tu' call which they use frequently. This allows their presence to be detected at long range and, as they are shy birds, before they are disturbed. They lay four off-white eggs, finely peppered reddish-brown.

summer    winter

## GREY PLOVER *Charadrius squatarola* ▶
**Length** 11 in (28 cm).
**Appearance** Adults in winter flecked grey, black-and-white above, white below with conspicuous black underwing patch or 'armpit' visible in flight. In summer face, breast and belly are black; back speckled silver-grey. Young resemble winter adults.
**Distribution** Winter visitor to north-west, west and southern coasts of Europe.

The bulky, short-beaked grey plovers often feed singly, dotted about the mudflats among close-packed flocks of other waders. Most can be seen around British, west and south European coasts in winter, when their plaintive piping 'tee-loo-ee' is easy to hear. In spring, late migrants from southern Africa, heading for their tundra breeding grounds in the Arctic, may be seen on our coasts in their spectacularly beautiful breeding plumage. The nest contains four eggs, which are buffish in colour with dark brown blotches.

winter    summer

## GOLDEN PLOVER *Pluvialis apricaria* ▶
**Length** 11 in (28 cm).
**Appearance** Winter adults dull gold above, flecked black-and-white; white below. Summer adults glowing gold above, with flecks; face, breast and belly black. Young birds resemble winter adults.
**Distribution** Breeds in north and north-west Europe (including Britain); winters in west, south-west and southern Europe.

With their handsome plumage, wild 'tlooee' call and rippling, fluting song, golden plovers are one of the most attractive of the moorland and mountain breeding birds of Britain and northern Europe. In winter, the breeding birds move to lower altitudes and are joined by migrants from the colder northern parts of the Continent. Some will stay on coastal marshes, but others may be seen in swift-flying flocks well inland: anywhere that there are wide expanses of unfrozen floodwater or lush grazing in undisturbed lowland river valleys. They lay four buff eggs with bold reddish blotches.

## TURNSTONE▶
*Arenaria interpres*

winter

**Length** 9 in (23 cm).
**Appearance** Winter adults white below, boldly patterned in black; white, brown and russet above. Summer adults retain the bold patterns, but the browns and russets are replaced by chestnut and orange. Young resemble winter adults.
**Distribution** Breeds in extreme northern Europe; winters on western coasts.

Although turnstones may be seen on any of the rocky, seasweed-covered coasts of Britain and northern Europe in all months of the year, most are winter visitors and those in summer are either non-breeders or late migrants on route to their Arctic breeding grounds. Turnstones have short, flat beaks, well adapted (as their name implies) for use as a shovel to overturn pebbles or seaweed in search of food such as maggots or small shrimps. They lay usually four olive-coloured eggs, which are heavily marked with dark brown spots and squiggles.

winter summer

## BLACK-TAILED GODWIT *Limosa limosa*▶
**Length** 16 in (40 cm).
**Appearance** Adults in summer are mottled brown and chestnut above, with cinnamon on head, neck and breast shading to white; barred-brown below; in all seasons black-and-white wing and tail patterns are conspicuous in flight.
**Distribution** Breeds in north and central Europe; winters in extreme west and south-west Europe.

Black-tailed godwits breed on damp grazing marshes, usually laying four eggs which are greenish with dark spots. Their striking plumage and strident calls as they mob intruders make them very conspicuous. Breeding numbers in western Europe are generally low, but in winter the numbers are augmented by birds from further east, when they are found on coasts or estuaries, plunging their long, straight beaks into the soft mud, sometimes up to their eyes, in their search of worms and shellfish.

winter

## ◀ BAR-TAILED GODWIT *Limosa lapponica*
**Length** 15 in (38 cm).
**Appearance** Adults in summer cinnamon above, flecked brown; cinnamon below, darkening to chestnut on belly. Winter adults and young mottled grey above, white below. White tail with several dark bars; no wing-bar visible.
**Distribution** Breeds in extreme northern Europe; winters in west and south.

Bar-tailed godwits breed on the Arctic tundra, and in western Europe only a few late spring migrants moving northwards or early-returning failed breeders are likely to be seen in summer plumage. In winter, numbers are far greater, and bar-tailed godwits are a conspicuous feature of many estuaries. Like the black-tailed godwit (_L. limosa_),

they probe deeply for food, but can be separated from them by their lack of conspicuous wing and tail patterns in flight, and by their slightly up-curved, extremely long beaks when at rest. The nest contains two to four greenish or olive eggs with small brown spots.

winter

**SPOTTED REDSHANK** _Tringa erythropus_ ▼
**Length** 12 in (30 cm).
**Appearance** Adults in summer sooty black, with scaly white or grey markings; legs blood-red. Young birds and winter adults are mottled grey-brown above, white below.
**Distribution** Breeds in extreme north of Europe; winters in Britain, west and south-west Europe, and the Mediterranean.

Their summer plumage is so unusual and conspicuous that spotted redshanks merit their colloquial name 'dusky redshank'. They are far less common and widespread birds than their slightly smaller relative the redshank (_T. totanus_), and mostly occur on passage in spring and autumn, though in warmer areas a few birds regularly overwinter on coastal marshes or estuaries. Longer-legged, they feed in deeper water than the redshank, often wading up to their 'waist'. They lack the redshank's white wing-bar and noisy behaviour, and have a distinctive 'tu-whit' call. Usually four eggs are laid; these are olive-green with dark brown spots.

◄ **KNOT** *Calidris canutus*
**Length** 10 in (25 cm).
**Appearance** Adults in summer rusty-red
beneath; scaly-brown, gold and black above.
Young and winter adults grey-brown above,
white below.
**Distribution** Winter visitor to west and south-
west European coasts (including Britain).

Knot are one of the most nondescript of our birds; of
medium size, medium bill length and dumpy build,
they have few striking characteristics, except their
habit of occurring in dense flocks. In winter, some
sheltered estuaries may often hold flocks of knot
tens of thousands strong. At high tide they often
stand at the water's edge – hence their specific name
*canutus* after King Canute. Late spring migrants,
heading north in summer plumage, are a distinctive
red colour, and much easier to identify. Knot lay
three or four greenish or olive eggs marked with fine
brown spots and streaks.

**PURPLE SANDPIPER** *Calidris maritima* ►
**Length** 8 in (20 cm).
**Appearance** Winter adults and young leaden-
grey above and on breast; paler on belly;
medium-length down-curved beak; pale eye-ring;
yellow legs. In summer, feathers of back and
breast have ochrous edges, giving a scaly effect.
**Distribution** Breeds in far north; winter visitor
to west and north-west coasts of Europe
(including Britain).

Purple sandpipers are characteristic birds of rocky
sea-coasts, rarely seen anywhere else. Their drab
plumage provides excellent camouflage against the
seaweed-draped rocks as they dodge nimbly about
among the breaking waves, picking off small
animals dislodged by the sea. If disturbed by a
particularly heavy wave, the flock (usually of ten to
twenty birds) skim off low over the water to safer
feeding, showing a faint white wing-bar and white
sides to a dark-centred rump. Although most purple
sandpipers are winter visitors, a few will spend the
summer months on British and Irish coasts. Usually
four greenish, olive or buff eggs are produced, which
are spotted and streaked dark brown.

**DUNLIN** *Calidris alpina*▲
**Length** 7 in (18 cm).
**Appearance** Summer adults bronze speckled with black above, white with dark streaks below except for the all-black belly; beak long, down-curved; legs greenish. Young and winter adults mottled greys and browns above, white below.
**Distribution** Breeds in north and north-west Britain and Europe; winters in west, south and south-west Europe.

winter

In winter, dunlin are by far the most numerous small waders on sandy and muddy coasts and estuaries, often occurring in flocks many thousands strong which look like wisps of smoke as they twist and turn in the distance, showing first white, then grey. Somehow, even though the flocks are densely packed, the birds have the reflexes to reform these aerial manoeuvres at high speed without collisions. In summer, most move north to the tundra to breed, but a sizeable breeding population nests on upland and coastal moorland in northern and western Britain and Europe, where their attractive song – a purring trill – is a pleasant feature of the summer. Usually four eggs are laid, brownish with darker spots in a dense spiral.

161

**CURLEW SANDPIPER** *Calidris ferruginea* ▶
**Length** 8 in (20 cm).
**Appearance** Summer adults chestnut above
and below, with brown wings; legs and long
down-curved beak blackish. Young and winter
adults mottled grey-brown above, white below.
**Distribution** Passage migrant across a broad
European front.

Regular visitors to fresh and salt water marshes, particularly near the coast, and to the mudflats of sheltered bays and estuaries, the curlew sandpipers seen in Britain and Europe are on passage; those seen in Britain in late spring are likely to be in breeding plumage, as may some of the first to return – probably failed breeding birds – in July. Although longer-billed and longer-necked, curlew sandpipers may sometimes be difficult to distinguish from the slightly smaller dunlin (*C. alpina*). In flight, the all-white rump and black tail of the curlew sandpipers are useful identification points, as are their whistling, bell-like chirrups, quite distinct from the dunlin's wheezy call. Curlew sandpipers usually lay four eggs, in a single clutch, and these are olive-brown with dark brown blotches.

**SANDERLING** *Calidris alba* ▶
**Length** 8 in (20 cm).
**Appearance** In winter, silver-grey above, with a
black mark through the eye and black beak and
legs. Summer adults pale chestnut above, with
cinnamon markings on breast.
**Distribution** Winter visitor to west, south-west
and south coasts of Europe.

Only rarely will summer plumage sanderlings be seen as they pass through in May on a late passage north to their Arctic breeding grounds. But in winter, the sanderling is both numerous and widespread on flat sandy beaches where little groups of them will dash along the shore, following receding waves out and then running in before the next, frequently pausing to pick up minute items of food disturbed by the water. Their legs move so quickly that they seem just a blur, and high speed photographs which freeze the action show both feet well clear of the ground! Sanderlings usually lay four olive-coloured eggs, sparsely spotted brown.

## AVOCET *Recurvirostra avosetta* ▲
**Length** 17 in (43 cm).
**Appearance** Unmistakeable; adults mainly white, with black crown and nape; black bars on back and wings, and black wing-tips; long slender upturned beak; long blue-grey legs. Young birds browner.
**Distribution** Breeds in parts of north-west Europe (including Britain), more common in southern Europe; winters in the west and south of Europe.

Although widespread and sometimes common on the Continent, especially round the Mediterranean, avocets had long been extinct as a breeding bird in Britain until disastrous east coast flooding in 1953 accidentally re-created their lost habitat. Since then, under the watchful and creative care of the Royal Society for the Protection of Birds (who adopted the bird as their emblem) breeding numbers of these elegant birds have increased at several sites. In winter, most migrate south but some remain on sheltered estuaries. Avocets normally lay three or four black-spotted buff eggs. When feeding, the avocet's upturned bill scythes from side to side across the water surface, picking up insects.

## BLACK-WINGED STILT ►
*Himantopus himantopus*
**Length** 15 in (38 cm).
**Appearance** Unmistakeable; adults white-bodied, with varying amounts of grey or black on nape; black back and wings; beak long and black; extremely long pink legs. Young birds brown above, with pale pink legs.
**Distribution** Summer visitor to south and south-west Europe.

Apart from the extraordinary length of their legs, which allows stilts to feed (pecking insects off the surface) in far deeper water than any other wader, they draw attention to themselves by hovering over any intruder, legs trailing, and yelping loudly. They are chiefly birds of Mediterranean saltpans, and only rare vagrants to Britain and Ireland. In the last 30 years, two isolated pairs have nested in England. Black-winged stilts lay between three and five buff eggs, with dark brown and grey blotches.

## RED-NECKED PHALAROPE▲
*Phalaropus lobatus*
**Length** 7 in (18 cm).
**Appearance** Summer adults mottled with browns and buffs above, with red neck; white below. Winter adults and young pale grey-brown above, white below, with dark smudge through the eye.

**Distribution** Breeds in extreme north and north-west of Europe (including Britain).

Red-necked phalaropes are rare birds over much of Europe, most often seen on inland marshy areas or passing by far out to sea following stormy autumn weather. They breed in Iceland and northern Scandinavia, and in Scotland and Ireland in small numbers, and are intriguing because the normal roles of the sexes are reversed. The female is larger and brighter than the male, and takes the lead in courtship. Once the four or so greenish eggs, heavily spotted with brown, are laid, the male incubates and then raises the brood alone, while the female seeks a fresh partner.

◄ **ARCTIC SKUA** *Stercorarius parasiticus*
**Length** 18 in (45 cm).
**Appearance** Adults in two plumage phases, both having characteristic dark wings with large white patches. Dark phase has all-chocolate-brown body; pale phase is buff below with dark cap; central tail feathers extend well beyond tail. Young birds mottled with pale browns; lack long tail feathers.
**Distribution** Breeds on extreme north and

164

north-west coasts of Europe (including parts of Britain); winters in tropical oceans.

Arctic skuas can be seen off many parts of western European coasts on migration in spring and autumn, as well as around the coasts and islands of Scandinavia and northern Scotland when breeding. Although capable of catching fish and other food for themselves, they tend to harass terns and the smaller gulls like kittiwakes, using their agility in the air to force these birds to drop or disgorge any food they are carrying. Once this has been achieved, the 'pirate' swoops to pick up its meal and its unfortunate victim returns to hunt for more food. The clutch usually contains two olive-coloured eggs with dark brown markings.

**GREAT SKUA** *Stercorarius skua*▶
**Length** 23 in (58 cm).
**Appearance** Adults and young dark brown, flecked with buff; wings darker, with conspicuous white patch.
**Distribution** Breeds in the extreme north-west of Europe (including Britain); winters in the Atlantic.

Huge and dark, with only slightly projecting central tail feathers, great skuas use their power and size (they are almost as large as a great black-backed gull) to carry out piratical attacks on gulls, terns and even gannets. If sheer aerial harassment does not succeed, the skua will seize one wing-tip and attempt to overturn a flying gannet, and this is usually enough to make it disgorge its fish. Great skuas are scarce breeding birds of the northern Scottish islands, and are very aggressive in defence of their nests – in which they lay two dark-spotted olive eggs – often actually striking human intruders while 'dive-bombing' them. They migrate south for the winter, and may be seen in any coastal waters in spring and autumn.

light phase

**POMARINE SKUA** ▶
*Stercorarius pomarinus*
**Length** 20 in (50 cm).
**Appearance** Two plumage phases: dark phase all dark brown, except for white wing-patches; pale phase white or buff below, with brown cap and collar; central tail feathers of adults elongated and twisted at tips. Young birds mottled honey-brown.
**Distribution** Breeds on the Arctic tundra; coastal migrant elsewhere.

Breeding on the Arcitc tundra, where they feed mainly upon lemmings, pomarine skuas are scarce birds over much of Europe. Most are seen off the coasts on spring or autumn passage, harrying gulls and terns in inshore waters. Good places to watch for these birds include promontories such as Portland Bill (Dorset), Dungeness (Kent) and Spurn Head (Yorkshire) and large bays, where gulls and terns regularly accumulate to shelter from rough weather or to feed. Up to three brown eggs with dark brown spots are laid, in a single clutch.

## GREAT BLACK-BACKED GULL ▶
*Larus marinus*
**Length** 27 in (68 cm).
**Appearance** Adults white, with black back and black wings with a white trailing edge; beak yellow with red spot; legs pink. Young birds white, mottled brown, gradually acquiring adult plumage over four years.
**Distribution** Breeds in north and north-west Europe (including Britain); winters on north, west and south coasts of Europe.

The largest of our gulls, great black-backed gulls choose rocky coasts on which to breed, often in single pairs rather than in colonies, unlike most of the gulls. They lay two or three buff or olive eggs, blotched with brown. Although fishing for some of their food, they prey heavily on the eggs, young and often even on the adults of other seabirds: storm petrels, manx shearwaters and puffins are common victims. In the winter months, some remain in coastal waters, while others forage far out to sea. Still others, usually immature birds, move inland and feed on urban refuse tips, roosting at night on nearby estuaries, lakes or reservoirs.

## ◀ LESSER BLACK-BACKED GULL
*Larus fuscus*
**Length** 21 in (53 cm).
**Appearance** Adults white, with slate-grey wings with black-and-white tips; beak yellow with red spots; legs yellow. Young birds mottled brown-and-white, gradually acquiring adult plumage over four years.
**Distribution** Breeds in north and north-west Europe (including Britain); winters west, south-west and central Europe.

Best distinguished from the larger great black-backed gull (*L. marinus*) and the similarly sized herring gull (*L. argentatus*) by their yellow, rather than pink legs, lesser black-backed gulls have a rather variable back colour. British breeding birds are relatively pale grey; Scandinavian ones are almost as dark as great black-backs. Lesser black-backs are migrants, most wintering off southern Europe and North Africa, although increasing numbers are overwintering in northern parts, exploiting the abundance of food contained in urban refuse tips. Breeding season numbers are increasing fast, and some colonies are tens of thousands of pairs strong. They lay two or three dark-spotted greenish-coloured eggs.

## HERRING GULL *Larus argentatus* ▲
**Length** 22 in (55 cm).
**Appearance** Adults white-bodied; silver-grey wings with black-and-white tips; beak yellow with red spot; legs pink. Young birds flecked dark brown, becoming paler and reaching adult plumage over four years.
**Distribution** Breeds on most British and European coasts; found inland in winter.

If sheer increase in numbers is an indication of success, then herring gulls – currently expanding their population at a phenomenal 10 per cent per annum – are clearly extremely successful birds. The majority breed on cliffs and rocky coasts, rocky islets or sand dunes, all in areas free from disturbance from man, but there are now several inland colonies in remote moorland areas and many instances of herring gulls nesting on rooftops in coastal towns, where two or three olive-green, dark-flecked eggs are laid. Their raucous 'dawn chorus' and liberal aerial bombardment of droppings on unsuspecting holidaymakers has led to a marked fall in the popularity of the 'seagull'. In the winter months they are widespread inland, many feeding on urban refuse tips.

## COMMON GULL *Larus canus* ▶
**Length** 16 in (40 cm).
**Appearance** Adults white with silver-grey, black-and-white-tipped wings; beak and legs yellowish or greenish. Young birds mottled in brown and white, acquiring adult plumage over two or three years.
**Distribution** Widespread summer visitor, breeding in many northern areas (including Britain); winters in the south, south-west and west of Euorpe.

Common gulls breed widely on the moorlands of northern Europe, ranging south to Scotland and Ireland, and occasionally further south, although the colony on the shingle banks at Dungeness in the south of England is an exception both in habitat choice and location. Many birds winter in southern European areas; some are found on the coast, but many remain on flooded pastures and farmland, and others frequent urban refuse tips, but perhaps less commonly than most other gulls. Two or three brown-blotched eggs are laid.

## ◄ MEDITERRANEAN GULL
*Larus melanocephalus*
**Length** 15 in (38 cm).
**Appearance** Summer adults have jet-black hood; white body; pale grey wings; heavy dark-banded orange beak. Winter adults lack dark head but have sooty mark through eye. Young birds have dark wings, brown on mantle and broad black band on tail.
**Distribution** Breeds in extreme south-east of Europe; winters around north-west and south-west Mediterranean.

Most Mediterranean gulls breed towards the eastern end of the Mediterranean or around the Black Sea, and venture to British and Irish coastal seas relatively rarely, and often as immature birds. They are slightly larger and heavier than black-headed gulls (*L. ridibundus*), and juveniles have much darker wing-tips. In recent years a few adults have bred in southern English counties, some of them pairing with black-headed gulls. Two to three pale olive eggs with dark brown spots are laid, in a single clutch.

## BLACK-HEADED GULL ►
*Larus ridibundus*
**Length** 14 in (35 cm).
**Appearance** Summer adults white with chocolate hood; grey wings with white leading edges; blood-red bill and legs. Winter adults lose brown hood. Young birds lack hood and have brown marks on back and wings, narrow black band on tail and black-tipped white flight feathers.
**Distribution** Breeds in Britain, north, west and central Europe; winters in west and central southern Europe.

One of the most abundant gulls year-round, black-headed gulls nest colonially in a variety of sites such as estuary islands, disused gravel pits, sand dunes and lochs and tarns high on the moors where they lay up to four dark-spotted olive-green eggs. At the turn of the century, they were almost unknown in towns, but now they are characteristic birds of park lakes and playing fields in winter. Their diet is varied, taking bread from the hand or searching for worms in waterlogged soil. Nor are they averse to scavenging on urban refuse during the winter months.

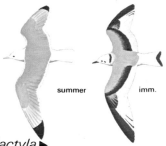

summer      imm.

**KITTIWAKE** *Rissa tridactyla* ▶
**Length** 16 in (40 cm).
**Appearance** Adults white-bodied; narrow grey wings tipped with black; beak yellow; legs black. Young similar, but with black collar, 'W' mark on wings, and black tip to tail.
**Distribution** Breeds on west, north and north-west coasts of Britain and Europe; winters in Atlantic.

Kittiwakes build their nests in colonies, usually on sheer cliffs often with a considerable overhang, cementing the platform on to the slightest of projections. Here they lay three sandy-grey eggs with dark blotches. One good definition of a kittiwake nest site would be that no other bird could nest there! The fledgling young disperse with the adults out into the open Atlantic for the winter. The kittiwake is an excellent example of a bird that calls its own name quite clearly, and raucous calls of 'kitti-wa-a-a-ke' readily lead the birdwatcher towards its breeding cliffs.

summer

**ARCTIC TERN** *Sterna paradisaea* ▶
**Length** 15 in (38 cm).
**Appearance** Summer adults black-capped and grey-winged – primaries almost translucent; white-bodied, with long tail streamers; short red legs; beak red. Young and winter adults have white forehead, brownish beak and legs.
**Distribution** Breeds in extreme north and north-west Europe (including Britain).

Arctic terns probably see more hours of daylight each year than any other creature. They breed in northern parts, as far as the Arctic Circle where the summer is virtually without nights. The nest contains one to three sandy olive eggs with dark spots. Having raised their young on the short-lived summer abundance of insects and fish fry, they migrate southwards along our coasts, crossing the Equator to spend our winter in the Antarctic Ocean. Here again there is almost perpetual daylight, and the terns can enjoy the immensely rich food supply of small fish and plankton which flourish during the Antarctic summer.

summer    winter    imm.

**COMMON TERN** *Sterna hirundo* ▶
**Length** 14 in (35 cm).
**Appearance** Summer adults with dark-tipped
red beak; red legs; black cap; grey upperparts and
a long forked tail; underparts white. Winter adults
have white forehead. Young have some brown
coloration in the wings.
**Distribution** Breeds in most parts of Britain
and Europe; winters in Africa.

Perhaps the most numerous of the British and Irish
terns, common terns are widespread European
summer visitors, wintering usually off Africa but
occasionally straying enormous distances; a ringed
bird was recovered in Australia. Terns hunt for their
food by flapping lazily along over shallow inshore
seas (and sometimes inland over fresh water) before
suddenly turning and plunging headlong, submerging briefly with an audible splash, to emerge with a
small fish grasped crosswise in the beak. Often this
will be taken back to the bird's mate or young in a
colony on an island, or on a remote sandy or marshy
coast. A few pairs now nest on man-made inland
habitats such as gravel pits, where they lay up to
four brown eggs with black blotches.

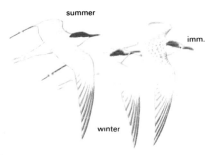

bristly crown; legs black; black beak with yellow tip. Winter adults have white forehead and crown. Young birds are mottled blackish.
**Distribution** Breeds on coasts of eastern Britain, and northern Europe.

Sandwich terns are summer visitors, and usually the first birds reach southern coasts in March. Breeding colonies, which may be thousands strong, are dotted about the coast on remote islands, lagoons, sand dunes or shingle spits. They are easily disturbed, and colonies often shift their position from year to year, occasionally even in mid-season. Up to three whitish brown-flecked eggs are laid.

**SANDWICH TERN** *Sterna sandvicensis* ▲
**Length** 16 in (40 cm).
**Appearance** Summer adults white below; white, shallowly forked tail; wings grey; black

---

**Distribution** Breeds around many of the coasts of Britain and Europe.

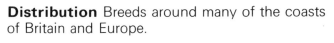

Although not at all difficult to spot fishing close inshore off many coastlines, little terns are one of our scarcer seabirds, declining rapidly in numbers. They are summer visitors, nesting on sandy beaches, and because of this suffer heavily from disturbance (much of it unintentional) by holiday-makers seeking deserted beaches. Their eggs and chicks are so well camouflaged that they may be trodden on inadvertently, and little terns have also to cope with natural hazards such as predators and stormy seas sweeping nests and eggs off the beach. Up to three dark-flecked sandy eggs are laid.

◄ **LITTLE TERN** *Sterna albifrons*
**Length** 9 in (23 cm).
**Appearance** Summer adults white below; grey above, with white forehead, dark crown and black-tipped yellow beak. Winter adults duller, with more white on crown. Young birds mottled with brown.

171

## RAZORBILL *Alca torda* ▶

**Length** 16 in (40 cm).

**Appearance** Summer adults jet-black above, with white line on wings and white lines on face and a heavy beak; underparts white. Winter adults and young greyer.

**Distribution** Breeds on the coasts of Britain and northern Europe; winters in Atlantic Ocean and North Sea.

Although they ride low in the water, when they are standing on the ledges of rocky cliffs on which they breed razorbills have an upright posture and resemble small versions of the extinct great auk. They have a rapid, whirring flight low over the water, with little evidence of aerodynamic skill, for they frequently land in rough weather with an undignified splash. Under water, however, they are fast and expert swimmers, using their stiff, stubby wings and their feet. The nest contains a single egg, often buff with dark blotches and squiggles.

## PUFFIN *Fratercula arctica* ▶

**Length** 12 in (30 cm).

**Appearance** Summer adults black above, with white face; white below; orange legs; huge red, blue- and yellow-banded beak. Young and winter adults dark grey above, smoky white below, with smaller dark beak.

**Distribution** Breeds in Britain and northern Europe; winters in Atlantic and North Sea.

Most puffin colonies are large, and sited on remote, nearly inaccessible coasts, for puffins are very sensitive to human disturbance. A single white egg is laid, and once the young have hatched in June, adults can often be seen visiting their burrows with small fish held crosswise in their beaks. Often there may be a dozen or more, but up to 60 small fry in one beakful have been recorded. It is still not clearly understood how the puffin manages to catch and hold so many fish. The huge parrot-like beak, so colourful in summer, is grown only for display in the breeding season. The horny outer sheath is lost at the end of summer, to be replaced by a much smaller, strictly functional grey beak, for the winter months out in the open seas.

## GUILLEMOT *Uria aalge* ▶
**Length** 16 in (40 cm).
**Appearance** Summer adults dark chocolate above (almost black in northern Europe), white below – some with white eye-ring and mark behind eye. Winter adults and young generally greyer.
**Distribution** Breeds in Britain and northern Europe; winters in Atlantic and North Sea.

One of our commonest seabirds, guillemots nest on cliff edges and the tops of rock stacks in suitable coastal areas, some remaining in coastal waters throughout the winter. The nest is non-existent and the single, large, darkly marked egg is simply laid, with many others, on a ledge. The egg is pear-shaped, and if knocked rolls in a tight circle, not off the ledge to its doom as would, say, a chicken's egg.

The great variation in colour is thought to be an aid to the homecoming adult returning from the sea, enabling it to identify its egg among many others on the ledge.

## ROCK/WATER PIPIT ▶
*Anthus spinoletta*
**Length** 6 in (15 cm).
**Appearance** Rock pipit dingiest of all the pipits; dark legs, upperparts and breast; dusky outer tail-feathers; streaks on the breast are inconspicuous. Water pipit has dark legs, white eye-stripe and outer tail feathers and, in summer, a pinkish flush on the unstreaked breast.
**Distribution** Rock pipits are resident in Britain and north-west Europe, wintering in western Europe; Water Pipits are southern European residents.

The various races or subspecies of this species fall into two main groups: rock pipits, which are confined to rocky coasts and islands; and water pipits, which breed in the mountains of central and southern Europe. Their dark plumage provides excellent camouflage as they search seaweed-covered rocks for small molluscs and insect larvae. This species is resistant to severe weather, and many individuals remain in the same locality throughout the year. However, between September and April, others wander to estuaries, saltings, muddy and sandy shores and various freshwater localities inland. Four or five brownish mottled eggs are laid, and there are two broods.

# Index